KEY SKILLS IN ENGLISH

Janna Tiearney

Fourth Class

Activity Book

gill & macmillan
g&m
primary

Introduction to Teachers and Parents

This book is one of a series of English Skills Books aimed at children in First to Sixth Class: 1, 2, 3, 4, 5 and 6. The *Lift Off!* series has been written by an experienced primary school teacher, Janna Tiearney who has devised a specific scheme of work on the teaching of core English skills in direct response to feedback from teachers around the country.

How to use this book

This book is self-contained and designed to be used independently by children alongside any core English programme. This book is laid out in a child-friendly manner and includes contemporary and engaging artwork and themes. The reading texts and exercises have been carefully graded and each book is a continuation and revision of the content of the previous book. The earlier books naturally place a greater emphasis on word sounds and phonics, while the later books focus more on grammar. All books contain a consistent format of activities to promote children's confidence. Each unit covers all three strands of the English curriculum: reading, writing and oral language. Each unit, in each book, consists of 6 pages. Each page carries its own *Friendly Owl* icon in the top corner of the page.

Page	Icon		Content
Page 1		Reading	Pre-reading question, illustration and reading text
Page 2		Reading & responding	'Talk about' topic, comprehension and higher order questions
Page 3		Sounds	Letter sounds and phonics activities using visual support
Page 4		Grammar	Activities including rules, examples, drill and practice questions
Page 5		Looking at words	Spelling activities using sight words from the reading section
Page 6		Extra optional page	Optional drama, personal writing and a fun puzzle section

Other features

- **'Before you read ...'** question: will capture the child's interest and give him/her a purpose for reading.
- **'Talk about'** oral language activities follow each reading piece encouraging children to engage fully with the text and create their own meaning.
- **Information bubbles** are dotted throughout the book for the purpose of fun, as points of information and to promote further thinking on the theme or given concept.
- **'Remember boxes'** are used throughout the grammar sections to assess and remind children of what they have learned already.
- **'Sample boxes'** provide the children with important, accessible examples to ensure they understand the grammar point before completing the task.
- **Revision pages** appear at key stages in the book to promote the revisiting and consolidation of letter sounds and crucial grammar points and as a means of assessing progress during the year.
- **Integrated activities within each unit:** The personal writing, sight words, and oral language activities are linked to the reading text. This means that the children are familiar with the topic by the time they come to write about it.
- **Comprehensive sight word list:** Each unit has a list of sight words that children can read in context. By completing the sight word activities in each unit, children are able to build up a comprehensive list of sight words, which they can then use in their own writing and reading.
- **Effective spelling strategies:** The 'Looking at words' page uses the *Look and say, picture, cover, write and check* method to teach spellings. A word list is provided and there are spaces to record the spellings and more spaces to correct any spelling mistakes. Other word recognition strategies have been included to encourage children to find the strategies that work best for them.

Fourth Class Activity Book
Contents

Unit 1	Reading: Pelorus Jack	2
	Reading: Activities	3
	Letter sounds: Digraphs	4
	Grammar: Capital letters, full stops and question marks	5
	Looking at words: front, years, colour, where, between, swimming, relief, guide, famous, anyone	6
	Extra! Extra! Drama, writing a description, making words	7
Unit 2	Reading: Hector the collector (poem)	8
	Reading: Activities	9
	Letter sounds: Digraphs	10
	Grammar: Capital letters (nationalities, acronyms), revision	11
	Looking at words: paper, half, wouldn't, bottles, shining, treasure, chairs, buckles, puzzles, handles	12
	Extra! Extra! Reciting and writing a poem, matching collectors	13
Unit 3	Reading: The panda bear	14
	Reading: Activities	15
	Letter sounds: Digraphs	16
	Grammar: Exclamation marks, revision	17
	Looking at words: bear, thick, leaves, types, wild, mouth, creature, kept, million, juice, parents	18
	Extra! Extra! Giving a description, researching and writing facts, word grid	19
Unit 4	Reading: Thank you letter (note, text message)	20
	Reading: Activities	21
	Letter sounds: Digraphs	22
	Grammar: Commas (in lists), revision	23
	Looking at words: aunt, busy, share, purple, unusual, kindness, wonderful, clothes, message, delighted, trousers	24
	Extra! Extra! Conversation, writing a note, matching text messages	25
Unit 5	Reading: Amusement centre flyer	26
	Reading: Activities	27
	Letter sounds: 'or' and 'ar' words	28
	Grammar: Prepositions	29
	Looking at words: medium, special, parties, adults, snacks, telephone, centre, ages, bowling, deposit, refreshments, opening	30
	Extra! Extra! Demonstrating an activity, making a flyer, quiz	31
Unit 6	Reading: Hans, the hero of Haarlem	32
	Reading: Activities	33
	Letter sounds: 'er', 'ir' and 'ur' words	34
	Grammar: Plurals	35
	Looking at words: country, lower, done, fields, screamed, town, idea, ache, frightened, didn't, felt, carrying	36
	Extra! Extra! Drama, writing for younger readers, coded message	37
Unit 7	Reading: The San Francisco earthquake	38
	Reading: Activities	39
	Letter sounds: 'or', 'ar', 'er' word endings	40
	Grammar: Revision (punctuation, prepositions, plurals)	41
	Looking at words: early, suddenly, earth, beneath, loud, everywhere, whatever, buildings, clouds, areas, earthquake, large, forever	42
	Extra! Extra! Role-play, writing a diary entry, the Richter scale	43
Unit 8	Reading: Two witches discuss good grooming (poem)	44
	Reading: Activities	45
	Letter sounds: Revision (digraphs, 'ar', 'er', 'ir', 'or', 'ur' words)	46
	Grammar: Nouns (common, proper, collective)	47
	Looking at words: teeth, mine, shade, daily, isn't, envy, brighten, just, failed, breath, secrét, natural, discuss	48
	Extra! Extra! Reciting and writing a poem, drawing	49
Unit 9	Reading: Pet column	50
	Reading: Activities	51
	Letter sounds: 'war' and 'wor' words	52
	Grammar: Verbs and adverbs	53
	Looking at words: fluffy, beautiful, service, lose, loving, advice, female, perfect, painless, monthly, loyal, prizes, support, ticket	54
	Extra! Extra! Role-play, writing an advert, word ladder	55
Unit 10	Reading: The five-coloured deer	56
	Reading: Activities	57
	Letter sounds: Letter patterns	58
	Grammar: Adjectives, comparative and superlative	59
	Looking at words: rare, forest, no-one, cried, coat, promise, reward, diamonds, receive, drowning, changes, deserves, word, pity	60
	Extra! Extra! Drama, writing a story, letter puzzle	61
Unit 11	Reading: Owls	62
	Reading: Activities	63
	Letter sounds: 'ch' words	64
	Grammar: Pronouns	65
	Looking at words: owls, nocturnal, during, except, insects, eagle, shelter, movements, quiet, prey, sites, edges, silently, hidden, trunks	66
	Extra! Extra! Reciting a poem, writing key words and facts, words within words	67
Unit 12	Reading: Grace Darling	68
	Reading: Activities	69
	Letter sounds: Prefixes	70
	Grammar: Homophones, revision	71
	Looking at words: weather, lighthouse, against, coast, daughter, worse, below, survive, rough, storm, England, warning, roared, steady, rescue	72
	Extra! Extra! Retelling the story, writing a story, wordsearch	73
Unit 13	Reading: The wolf's excuse (poem)	74
	Reading: Activities	75
	Letter sounds: Suffixes	76
	Grammar: Revision (nouns, verbs, adjectives, adverbs, punctuation)	77
	Looking at words: excuse, wolf, greed, hungry, leather, chewed, fate, care, cottage, eaten, shouldn't, bait, tender, believe, knocking	78
	Extra! Extra! Making excuses, writing a poem, spoonerisms	79
Unit 14	Reading: Babysitting instructions	80
	Reading: Activities	81
	Letter sounds: Revision (prefixes, suffixes, letter patterns)	82
	Grammar: Apostrophes (ownership)	83
	Looking at words: chicken, babysitting, vegetables, watch, television, fighting, ground, remove, nightmares, hotel, mobile, allow, microwave, dinner, climb	84
	Extra! Extra! Giving and writing instructions, changing words	85
Unit 15	Reading: How Rome got its name	86
	Reading: Activities	87
	Letter sounds: Silent letters	88
	Grammar: Speech marks	89
	Looking at words: twins, evil, uncle, basket, babies, protected, growl, agreed, terrible, rage, powerful, floated, threw, taken, heavy	90
	Extra! Extra! Drama, writing about an imaginary town, matching place names	91
Unit 16	Reading: Food labels	92
	Reading: Activities	93
	Letter sounds: 'wa' words	94
	Grammar: Past tense	95
	Looking at words: sauce, cooking, gently, stirring, spread, sugar, powder, wheat, protein, iron, fibre, energy, information, boil, oils	96
	Extra! Extra! Talking about and designing a label, spot the differences	97
Unit 17	Reading: Sky in the pie (poem)	98
	Reading: Activities	99
	Letter sounds: Revision ('ch' words, letter patterns, word endings)	100
	Grammar: Revision (apostrophes, speech marks, past tense)	101
	Looking at words: simply, sunsets, ordered, chef, artist, universe, spoonful, suppose, blend, flavour, hint, delicious, taste, polish, waiter	102
	Extra! Extra! Reciting and writing a poem, anagrams	103
Unit 18	Reading: Fionn and the Fianna	104
	Reading: Activities	105
	Letter sounds: Revision (silent letters, suffixes, prefixes)	106
	Grammar: Revision (past tense, apostrophes, speech marks, punctuation)	107
	Looking at words: warrior, certain, breaking, poetry, obey, whoever, thumb, knowledge, wise, fearful, burnt, music, leader, awake, happened	108
	Extra! Extra! Drama, writing a series of tests, following instructions	109

Do you know of a story where an animal has helped a person?

1. **Read the text.**

Pelorus Jack

He was first spotted by humans when he appeared in 1888 in front of a ship sailing between the North and South Islands of New Zealand. To the passengers amazement, the dolphin started to guide the ship through the narrow channel. This channel is dangerous as it has many rocks and reefs and fast flowing currents. For years after this the clever dolphin safely guided almost every ship that came by. He was so reliable that ships would look out for him and wait until he appeared.

Jack was a Risso's dolphin which is rare in New Zealand waters. He was pale in colour with a white head. He was named Pelorus Jack because the stretch of water where he lived was called the Pelorus Sound.

On one sad occasion, a passenger on board a ship named the *Penguin* shot at Pelorus Jack. The crew and passengers were furious when they saw the dolphin swimming away with blood flowing from him. For the next few weeks the dolphin was not seen and people were sure he had died. But one day Pelorus Jack re-appeared and he seemed to have recovered from his injuries. To everyone's relief he started once again to guide ships through the channel. However, if he saw the *Penguin* he would disappear. The *Penguin* was later wrecked and many passengers and crew drowned. This happened as it sailed through the channel unguided by Pelorus Jack.

For over twenty years this special dolphin led ships safely through these dangerous waters. He became so famous and so useful that the government of New Zealand passed a law forbidding anyone to capture or injure him.

Pelorus Jack was last seen in April 1912. It is believed that he died from old age.

2. **Talk about.**

   Talk about how animals help humans.

3. **Answer the questions.**

    Write full sentences.

   a. When did Pelorus Jack first appear?

   _____

   b. Why was the dolphin named Pelorus Jack?

   _____

   c. Where did he appear?

   _____

   d. What did the dolphin do?

   _____

   e. How did he get injured?

   _____

   f. What happened to the *Penguin*?

   _____

   g. For how many years did Pelorus Jack guide ships?

   _____

   h. When was he last seen?

   _____

4. **Write the answers in your copybook.**

   a. Why was the channel dangerous?

   b. Did Pelorus Jack help the *Penguin*? Explain.

   c. Do you think the government of New Zealand was pleased with the work Pelorus Jack did? Say why.

   d. Write a sentence about what you think about Pelorus Jack.

5. **Find words in the story with the same meaning. Use a dictionary**

   a. seen _____

   b. not common _____

   c. people travelling on a ship _____

   d. got better _____

   e. catch _____

   f. banning _____

   g. very angry _____

   h. well-known _____

6. Write the missing letters. Write out the full sentences.

oi	oy

a. The __ __ster holds a pearl.

_____

b. Do not touch that p__ __son.

_____

c. It is your ch__ __ce which book you want.

_____

d. My brother likes to ann__ __ me.

_____

e. You will destr__ __ the garden with that bike.

_____

7. Write the missing letters. Write out the full sentences.

ou	ow

a. Can you c__ __nt to a million?

_____

b. The cr__ __d went wild at the rock concert.

_____

c. We went in a gr__ __p to the movies.

_____

d. The king should wear a cr__ __n.

_____

e. That w__ __nd looks painful.

_____

8. Write the missing letters. Write out the full sentences in your copybook.

au	aw

a. Some people like to eat pr__ __ns.
b. The v__ __lt was full of money.
c. It's not my f__ __lt that I am late.
d. There was a br__ __l at the football match.
e. The rocket will l__ __nch at 3.00pm.

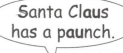
Santa Claus has a paunch.

9. Write six sentences in your copybook using words with each of these sounds.

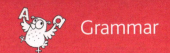

Capital letters are used at the beginning of a sentence.
Capital letters are also used for names, places, days of
the week, months, special days and titles.
Sentences end with a full stop.
Questions end with a question mark.

Will you be
my Valentine?

10. Underline the letters that should be capitals.
    Rewrite the sentences in your copybook.

   a.   fred goes to sweden every december to spend christmas with his cousins.

   b.   which school does james white go to?

   c.   on tuesdays and thursdays colm goes to belfast to visit aunt polly.

   d.   why is jemma laughing so loudly at larry's joke?

   e.   every april matthew tries to glimpse the easter bunny.

   f.   this morning it was bright and sunny mark and
       i went for a walk.

   g.   she had a farm in county mayo she had many animals
       to look after.

   h.   adam made pancakes on shrove tuesday they tasted salty.

11. Write three proper nouns for each group. Remember the capital letters.

towns			
surnames			
boys' names			
months			
special days			

12. Rewrite this paragraph in your copybook,
    adding capital letters and full stops.

   lions, along with tigers, are the biggest members of the cat
family lions used to live through much of europe and asia.
now they live in east and southern africa lions are hunters
and lionesses do most of the hunting male lions have
manes that usually get darker with age lions spend about
twenty hours a day sleeping and resting.

Word list

front	years	colour	where	between
swimming	relief	guide	famous	anyone

13. Learn the spellings. Now look and say, picture, cover, write, check.

_____   _____

_____   _____

_____   _____

_____   _____

14. Write any words you got wrong.

_____

15. Write the missing words. Use the word list.

   a.   The teacher stands at the _____ of the classroom.

   b.   Does _____ know where my runners are?

   c.   Navy blue is my favourite _____.

   d.   We can split the cost of the meal
        _____ the two of us.

   e.   Debbie wants to go _____ with dolphins.

16. In your copybook use these words to make sentences of your own:
    famous, **where**, **years**, **relief** and **guide**.

17. Write the answers. Use the word list.

   a.   Write the words from the list that have an **ou** pattern.

        _____

        Do they sound the same? _____

   b.   Break **anyone** into two words.

        _____   _____

   c.   Count the number of syllables in each word.

        between _____   **front** _____

        swimming _____   **years** _____

   d.   Which words contain these words?

        here _____   **ear** _____   **on** _____   **lie** _____

   e.   Which words have double letters? _____

   f.   Write a noun from the list. _____

One day
I will
be **famous**.

Drama

18. Work with a group. Pretend to be a sea creature. The group must guess what you are.

Write about

19. Imagine you have seen Pelorus Jack from on board a ship. Write what you saw. Read your description to a friend.

> Before you write, think about the following:
> - Where were you when you saw the dolphin?
> - What did it look like?
> - What was it doing?
> - How did you feel when you saw it?
>
> Use describing words.

_____
_____
_____
_____
_____
_____
_____

> Having pets is supposed to be good for our health. Loving a pet could calm us down and lower our blood pressure!

20. How many words can you make from this word?

> BOTTLE-NOSED DOLPHIN

_____
_____
_____
_____
_____

 Before you read...

Are you a collector of anything?

1. **Read the poem.**

Hector the collector

Hector the Collector
Collected bits of string,
Collected dolls with broken heads
And rusty bells that would not ring.
Pieces out of picture puzzles,
Bent-up nails and ice-cream sticks,
Twists of wires, worn out tyres,
Paper bags and broken bricks.
Old chipped vases, half shoelaces.
Gatlin' guns that wouldn't shoot,
Leaky boats that wouldn't float
And stopped-up horns that wouldn't toot.
Butter knives that had no handles,
Copper keys that fit no locks,
Rings that were too small for fingers,
Dried-up leaves and patched-up socks.
Worn-out belts that had no buckles,
'Lectric trains that had no tracks,
Airplane models, broken bottles,
Three-legged chairs and cups with cracks.
Hector the Collector
Loved these things with all his soul –
Loved them more than shining diamonds,
Loved them more than glistenin' gold.
Hector called to all the people,
'Come and share my treasure trunk!'
And all the silly sightless people
Came and looked .... And called it junk.

Shel Silverstein

2. **Talk about.**

   What kind of person do you think Hector was?
   Give reasons for your answer.

3. **Answer the questions.**

   a. What interest did Hector have?

   _____

   b. Name two types of toys he had collected.

   _____

   c. Name an item of clothing he had.

   _____

   d. What was wrong with the rings he had?

   _____

   e. Name two broken items he had collected.

   _____

   f. Who wrote the poem?

   _____

4. **Write the answers.**

   a. Why do you think Hector collected these things?

   _____

   b. How did Hector feel about the things?

   _____

   c. Why do you think he wanted to show other people his collection?

   _____

   d. What did the people think of Hector's collection?

   _____

   e. How do you think Hector felt about their reaction?

   _____

5. **Write the meanings of these words.**

   a. worn-out   _____
   b. chipped   _____
   c. 'lectric   _____
   d. airplane   _____
   e. gatlin' gun _____
   f. glistenin'   _____

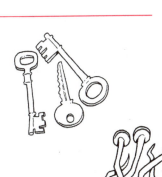

6. Write the missing letters.
   Write out the full sentences.

I need a **few** of you to make this **stew**.

| oo | ew | ue |

a. My cousin is my mother's neph___ ___.

_____

b. The flowers are in full bl___ ___m.

_____

c. The aven___ ___ is lined with trees.

_____

7. Write the missing letters.

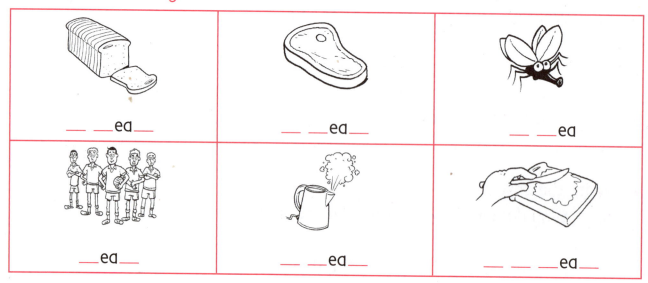

___ ___ea___   ___ ___ea___   ___ ___ea

___ea___   ___ ___ea___   ___ ___ ___ea___

8. The **ea** letters can make different sounds. Sort the words by their sound.

| dream | steak | spread | neat | please |
| deaf | great | bean | breath | cream |

ea as in break	**ea** as in meat	**ea** as in bread

9. Write six sentences in your copybook using words with sounds from this page.

Capital letters are also used for adjectives that are formed from proper nouns.

Sample I love Belgian chocolate.

Dutch cheese is best.

10. Form adjectives from these proper nouns.

a.	Germany	_____	h.	France	_____
b.	Sweden	_____	i.	Switzerland	_____
c.	Italy	_____	j.	Russia	_____
d.	Ireland	_____	k.	Denmark	_____
e.	Poland	_____	l.	Spain	_____
f.	Latvia	_____	m.	Scotland	_____
g.	Portugal	_____	n.	Norway	_____

11. Add capital letters and full stops to these sentences.
Rewrite them correctly in your copybook.
a. last friday we started our easter holidays
b. in america, on september the 9th, it is teddy bear day
c. durban and cape-town are cities in south africa
d. the most spoken language in the world is chinese
e. ludwig von beethoven was a german composer
f. the spanish coast is a popular holiday destination for the irish
g. the polish boy arrived in ireland on st. patrick's day
h. this belgian chocolate is the best i have ever tasted

Acronyms are made up of the initial letters of a phrase.

Sample United Nations = UN

Capital letters are also used for acronyms that are formed from proper nouns.

Sample UK = United Kingdom

12. Write acronyms for the following.
a. The United States of America _____
b. European Union _____
c. Gaelic Athletic Association _____
d. Unidentified Flying Object _____
e. Electricity Supply Board _____
f. Allied Irish Banks

Word list

paper	half	wouldn't	bottles	shining	treasure
chairs	buckles	puzzles	handles		

13. Learn the spellings. Now look and say, picture, cover, write, check.

_____   _____

_____   _____

_____   _____

_____   _____

14. Write any words you got wrong.

_____

15. Write the missing words. Use the word list.

a.   The moon is _____ in the night sky.

b.   Thirty-two is _____ of sixty-four.

c.   Try to recycle your glass and
     plastic _____ .

d.   I _____ be cheeky to adults.

e.   The _____ on your shoe will scratch the leather chair.

> How many **buckles** on your boots?

16. In your copybook use these words to make sentences of your own:
    paper, **treasure**, **chairs**, **puzzles** and **handles**.

17.   Write the answers. Use the word list.

a.   Write this word in full.   **wouldn't** _____

b.   Underline the silent letters in these words.   **half   puzzles**

c.   Write the root words of these words. (Remember: A root word is the
     smallest form of a word, e.g. the root word of **dancing** is **dance**.)

     collected _____   **shining** _____

     buckles _____   **handles** _____

d.   Break these words into syllables. Write the number of syllables
     for each.

     shining _____   **paper** _____

     treasure _____   **chairs** _____

e.   Write the words that have double letters. _____

f.   Underline the letter pattern that is the same in these words:
     buckles   puzzles   handles.

Talk about

18 Work with a group. Recite and discuss the poem *Hector the collector*.

Write about

19. In your copybook write a diamante poem about *Hector the collector*. Follow the example.

A DIAMANTE is a poem in the shape of a diamond. Diamante poems are seven lines long. Write your words in the middle of the line so that the poem is in the shape of a diamond.

Example

Teacher
caring and diligent
talking, marking, praising
blackboard, red pen, paper, books
explaining, reading, smiling
helpful, friendly
mentor.

Line 1. Noun
Line 2. Two adjectives
Line 3. Three 'ing' verbs
Line 4. Four nouns
Line 5. Three 'ing' verbs
Line 6. Two adjectives
Line 7. Noun

20. Match up the people with the things that they collect.

lepidopterist	collector of films
notaphilist	collector of stamps
oologist	collector of pearls
philatelist	collector of butterflies or moths
porcelainist	collector of bank notes
antiquarian	collector of teddy bears
pernalogist	collector of hi-fi equipment
cinephile	collector of birds' eggs
audiophile	collector of antiques
arctophilist	collector of porcelain

21. Can you name any other types of collectors? _____

_____

22. What would you like to collect? _____

_____

What kinds of bears do you know?

1. Read the text.

The panda bear

The panda bear, or giant panda as it is also called, lives in China. It is a black and white bear with a thick, woolly coat.

99% of the panda's diet is bamboo. Bamboo is not very nutritious. The shoots and leaves are the most valuable parts. There are many types of bamboo and a panda has to eat at least two different types or it will starve. It will also eat fish, small birds and rodents. The panda eats fast and often. It eats sitting up, pushing bamboo into its mouth twelve hours a day. It holds the bamboo with its front paws which have an extra 'thumb'. This 'thumb' is actually a larger wrist bone that sticks out and acts as a thumb to help the panda grip its food. The panda has molars that are flat and broad. This helps the animal to crush the bamboo.

The panda is a solitary creature, which means that it lives alone most of the time. Pandas are shy creatures and keep away from people.

Pandas are kept in just a few zoos around the world as keeping pandas is very costly. It costs more than two million euro per year. The pandas have state-of-the-art areas with 24-hour video monitoring, devoted keepers and vets, a plentiful supply of fresh bamboo to eat, together with carrots, yams and special vitamin cookies. Keepers even add chunks of fruit to juice and water, and then freeze the mix into 'Popsicles' as treats for the pandas. The pandas are also given a variety of toys to crush, wrestle, toss and roll. Many people flock to zoos to see pandas and one of the panda web cams in Washington Zoo attracts about two million visits a month!

In 2005 a baby panda called Tai Shan was born in Washington Zoo. This was the first offspring of parents Tian Tian and Mei Xiang.

There are probably less than 1000 pandas left in the wild. This is because of hunting and the cutting down of forests. Pandas are now a protected species.

> The panda bear can live 20 – 30 years in captivity.

2. **Talk about.**

    How can we help wildlife in our gardens?

3. **Answer the questions.**

    a.   Where does the panda bear live?

    _____

    b.   What is its main source of food?

    _____

    c.   What is the panda's extra 'thumb'?

    _____

    d.   Why do only a few zoos keep pandas?

    _____

    e.   Name one zoo that keeps pandas.

    _____

    f.   Why have panda numbers decreased?

    _____

4. **Complete the sentences.**

    a.   The panda bear is also called the _____.

    b.   It has to eat at least two _____ types of bamboo.

    c.   The flat and broad _____ help the panda to crush its food.

    d.   Tian Tian and Mei Xiang are _____ of Tai Shan.

    e.   In the zoos, the _____ treat the pandas with special care.

    f   The panda has a _____, _____ coat.

5. **Answer these questions in your copybook.**

    a.   Are pandas treated well in the zoos? Explain.

    b.   Why do you think they are such popular creatures?

    c.   What do you think of panda bears?

6. **Find words in the story with the same meaning. Use a dictonary.**

    a.   baby, child -   _____

    b.   die from hunger -   _____

    c.   back teeth -   _____

    d.   lives alone -   _____

    e.   faithful, loyal -   _____

    f.   nourishing -   _____

7. Write the missing letters. Write out the full sentences.

> ei   eigh   ay   ai   ey

a. The queen will r__ __gn over her country.   *Use your dictionary.*

_____

b. Do you like pl__ __ing cricket?

_____

c. My n__ __ __ __bour is quite nosy.

_____

d. That mud will st__ __n your shirt.

_____

e. Miss Muffet ate curds and wh__ __.

_____

8. Write the missing letters. Write out the full sentences.

> ee   ey   ei   ie

The rule is: 'i before e, except after c' when it sounds like bee.

a. The ch__ __f of the tribe was strong.

_____

b. There is a spider on the c__ __ling.

_____

c. The troll__ __ was full of groceries.

_____

d. Did you gr__ __t the teacher today?

_____

e. I would like a br__ __f word with you.

_____

9. Write the missing letters. Write out the full sentences in your copybook.

> igh   ie

*I **sigh**ed when I saw the size of the p**ie**.*

a. The fl__ __ __t to Spain took two hours.
b. Rachel has a sl__ __ __t pain in her knee.
c. Twenty-four blackbirds were baked in a p__ __.
d. You should be able to t__ __ your own shoelaces.
e. The vampire gave me a fr__ __ __t.

10. Write six sentences in your copybook using words with the sounds on this page.

Exclamation marks are used to show surprise or anger.

> **Sample** It was brilliant!

They are also used when someone is shouting or giving a command.

> **Sample** Stop it! Leave him alone!

Mum gave me roast beef for breakfast!

11. Write the sentences and finish them with a full stop, a question mark or an exclamation mark.

    a.   The cat had chicken for dinner! _____

    b.   Please hurry up. _____

    c.   How has your day been? _____

    d.   That is wonderful news! _____

    e.   Where has Shane gone? _____

    f.   When are you coming to visit? _____

    g.   Stop talking! _____

    h.   I have two younger brothers. _____

12. Add punctuation marks. (**!** . **?**)

Look out

Why, what's wrong

There's a lion behind you

Are you joking

No

Does he look friendly

He's opening his mouth

13. Add capital letters, full stops, question marks and exclamation marks to these sentences. Rewrite them correctly in your copybook.

    a.   go and tidy your room this minute

    b.   they say american burgers are the best

    c.   i got my dog sandy from the ispca

    d.   did you see the latvian girl on monday

    e.   get out of that tree now

    f.   lough neagh is the largest lake in ireland

    g.   where did ken put my irish homework

    h.   there's an alien outside

Word list

bear	thick	leaves	types	wild	mouth
creature	kept	million	juice	parents	

14. Learn the spellings. Now look and say, picture, cover, write, check.

_____   _____
_____   _____
_____   _____
_____   _____
_____   _____

15. Write any words you got wrong.

_____

16. Write the missing words. Use the word list.

a. In Autumn the _____ fall off the trees.

b. A koala bear, although cute, is a _____ animal.

c. Never approach a grizzly _____.

d. My _____ are lucky to have me for a child.

e. Do not chew with your _____ open.

f. There are many _____ of reading books.

17. In your copybook use these words to make sentences of your own:
million, **thick**, **creature**, **kept** and **juice**.

> You will write out a **million** lines if you don't stop talking.

18. Write the answers. Use the word list.

a. Find smaller words in these words from the list.
bear _____   **mouth** _____   **million** _____

b. Count the number of syllables in each word.
creature _____ **million** _____ **parents** _____ **juice** _____

c. Which words are in plural form?
(Remember: Plural means more than one.)

_____

d. Write words with an **ea** letter pattern.

_____

e. Do they sound the same? _____

f. Change one letter in each of these words to make words from the list.
trick _____   **month** _____   **wind** _____

Talk about

19. Work with a friend. Think of an imaginary animal and give it a name. Tell your friend as many details about the animal as possible.

What is the name of your animal? _____

Write about

20. Research a wild animal you are interested in. Write the facts in your copybook.

Think about:
- Where does it live?
- What is its diet?
- What does it look like?
- Does it have any distinguishing features?
- What other interesting facts did you learn about this animal?
- Why did you choose this animal?

Include a bibliography. This is a list of books and/or websites you used to get your information.

21. Tell the class about the animal your researched.

The World Wildlife Fund has the panda as its logo.

22. Fill in the endangered species grid. (Do not use the words in brackets.)

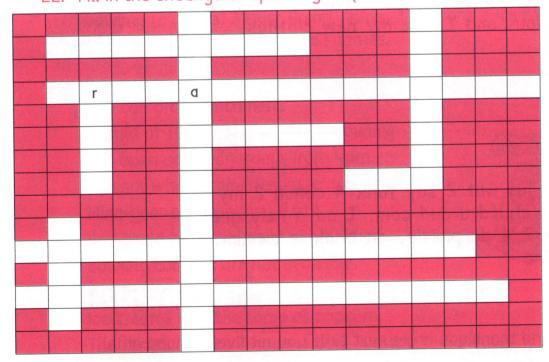

1. pignosed turtle
2. leaftailed gecko
3. tiger
4. elephant
5. (Asian) yew trees
6. irawaddy dolphin
7. ramin (tropical tree)
8. (sperm) whale
9. (Indiana) bat
10. great white shark

 When should we send thank you letters?

1. Read the thank you letters and notes.

THANK YOU

Dear Aunt Mary,

I would just like to take this opportunity to thank you for attending my birthday party. I know that you are very busy and I am delighted that you could share this occasion with me.

Thank you, too, for the unusual purple knitted trousers. They will keep me very warm in the winter.

Your kindness is much appreciated.
Your niece,
Claire

Formal

Dear Mum,

Thanks for letting me have a birthday party. I had a wonderful day. The cake you baked was delicious and I love my new clothes.

Love you!
Claire

Informal

Hi paddy jus wnt 2 say tanx 4 comin 2 my party. im chufd u cud com. I ad a rely gret dy. Tanx 2 4 da presie. da book is awsum.
Cya, Claire

Text message

Send thank you notes next time you receive birthday gifts!

2. Talk about.

When should we write formal letters?
What is the difference between formal and informal?

3. Answer the questions.

a.   Who had a birthday?

_____

b.   What did Aunt Mary give her?

_____

c.   Who gave Claire a book?

_____

d.   What did Claire's Mum make?

_____

e.   Do you think Claire enjoyed the party? Support your answer with a quote. (**Remember:** A quote is one or more words taken from the text. You need to use quotation marks.)

_____

f.   What is the best present you have ever received?

_____

4. Write the text message using full sentences. You can add and change words.

> Hi paddy. jus wnt 2 say tanx 4 comin 2 my party. im chufd u cud com. I ad a rely gret dy. Tanx 2 4 da presie. da book is awsum. Cya, Claire

_____

_____

_____

_____

5. Match the formal and the informal sentences.

Thank you for attending my party.   Hope to catch up with you later.
I am delighted you could come.   Thanks for the pressie.
My day was superb.   Glad you could make it.
Your gift is appreciated.   Had a great day.
I look forward to seeing you soon.   Thanks for comin'.

21

6. Write the missing letters. Write out the full sentences.

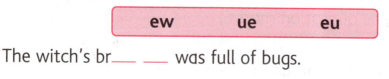

| ow | oe | oa |

Use a dictionary

a.   I can't talk as my thr__ __t is sore.

_____

b.   You are a friend not a f__ __.

_____

c.   Do not thr__ __ that sn__ __ball at me.

_____

d.   A d__ __ is female deer.

_____

e.   You should not b__ __st about how good you are.

_____

7. Write the missing letters. Write out the full sentences.

| ew | ue | eu |

a.   The witch's br__ __ was full of bugs.

_____

b.   Ireland is in __ __rope.

_____

c.   The cr__ __ on the ship were seasick.

_____

d.   I will contin__ __ with my work in a minute.

_____

e.   Use a tiss__ __ to blow your nose.

_____

8. Write the missing letters. Write out the full sentences in your copybook.

| ei | ea | ey | ie |

a.   Did you rec__ __ve your gift yet?
b.   Br__ __kfast is an important meal.
c.   I eat hon__ __ on toast.
d.   There are rabbits in the f__ __ld.
e.   I bel__ __ve there are aliens in my garden.

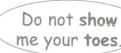

Do not **show** me your **toes**.

9. Write six sentences in your copybook using words that have the sounds on this page.

Commas are used between items in a list.

> **Sample** The monster was huge, smelly, green and hungry.
> There is no comma before **and.**

10. Add commas. Write the new sentences in your copybook.

    a. Wendy bought apples, pears, grapes and bananas.

    b. You must bring towels clothes food and a hat.

    c. At home I have dogs, cats, and cows.

    d. At night, I sleep with a cuddly, soft, cute teddy, bear.

    e. The house was cold, damp, musty, and spooky.

    f. He walked across the cold, frosty, and sparkling field.

    g. Africa has wild animals such as hippos, lions rhinos, giraffes and zebras.

    h. Do I have to wash my trousers, jumper, socks vest and underwear?

11. Complete the sentences using lists. Do not forget the commas!

    a. My Dad needs _____

_____.

    b. For my birthday I want _____

_____.

    c. The dog eats _____

_____.

    d. In my schoolbag you will find _____

_____.

    e. On my sandwich I would like _____

_____.

12. Add capital letters, full stops and commas to
these sentences. Rewrite them correctly in your copybook.

    a. you must eat your carrots, beans corn and broccoli.

    b. kirsty has long, curly, brown hair.

    c. i can't wait to break up on friday.

    d. in our school we have irish english and polish pupils.

    e. steve is getting clothes, books, socks and games
for his birthday in february.

> The teacher explains, talks, laughs, reads and yells!

23

Word list

aunt	busy	share	purple	unusual	kindness
wonderful	clothes	message	delighted	trousers

13. Learn the spellings. Now look and say, picture, cover, write, check.

_____   _____

_____   _____

_____   _____

_____   _____

_____

14. Write any words you got wrong.

_____

15. Write the missing words. Use the word list.
    a. The teacher was _____ with our good work.
    b. If you mix red and blue you will get _____.
    c. Leave a _____ for Mum when you go out.
    d. I hope you will _____ those sweets with me.
    e. My Dad's sister is my _____.
    f. Leah has been a _____ friend to me.

16. In your copybook use these words to make sentences of your own:
    unusual, **busy**, **kindness**, **clothes** and **trousers**.

My **trousers** keep falling down.

17. Write the answers. Use the word list.
    a. Find smaller words in these words from the list:
       clothes _____ **message** _____
       trousers _____ **busy** _____
    b. Count the number of syllables in each word:
       kindness _____ **wonderful** _____ **delighted** _____
    c. Which word from the list has a **silent e**? _____
    d. Which part of the word **unusual** makes it the opposite of **usual**?

       _____
    e. Which word has a **soft g**? _____
    f. Write the root words of these words:
       wonderful _____ **kindness** _____

Talk about

18. Work with a group. Act out a scene where friends talk using informal language or slang. Then try having a similar conversation using formal language and without any slang!

> Use formal language when writing to people you do not know personally.

Write about

19. In your copybook write a note to your teacher from your parents explaining why your homework has not been done. Use formal language. Be creative!

> Tips for writing formal language:
> - Never use slang or abbreviations.
> - Use good vocabulary and grammar.
> - Make sure you use capital letters, full stops, commas etc.
> - Never use exclamation marks.

> I don't suggest you use mobile text when you are writing at school!

20. Write the formal version of the following text messages.

> forever, thanks, have a nice day, tomorrow, sorry, keep in touch, got to go, dinner, anyone, do you remember, date, see you later, easy, if you say so, please

2MORO	_____	KIT	_____
DUR	_____	EZ	_____
GTG	_____	DNR	_____
HAND	_____	IFSS	_____
NE1	_____	D8	_____
CUL8R	_____	THX	_____
4EVA	_____	SRY	_____
PLS	_____		

21. Write your own text message.

_____

_____

Before you read...

Have you ever tried bowling?

1. Read the flyer.

Galaxy Amusement Centre

Main Street, Ballywater

Bowling
Entertainment for all ages
Wheelchair friendly
Lightweight balls for young children
Bowling coaches available
Special deals for birthday parties
Cost: per game: €5 adults   €3 children (under 12)

Games arcade
All games cost €2 per game

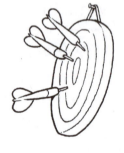

Pool and snooker
€15 deposit, €6 per hour

Darts (over 12s only)
€6 deposit, €3 per hour

Snacks and refreshments
Soft drinks: €2
Slush puppy: medium €2 large €3
Popcorn: €3
Crisps: €1.50
Ice-creams: €3

OPENING HOURS: TUESDAY TO SUNDAY
4.00PM – 12.00 PM
TELEPHONE: 055-1555444

2. **Talk about.**

Which activities at the amusement centre would you enjoy? Talk about fun things to do in your town.

3. **Answer the questions.**

a. What is the flyer advertising?

_____

b. How much per hour does it cost to play darts?

_____

c. Which activity requires a €15 deposit?

_____

d. Where is the centre?

_____

e. How much does it cost to play snooker for two hours?

_____

f. What time does the centre close?

_____

4. **Answer the questions in your copybook.**

a. Can young children go bowling? Explain your answer.

b. How many days of the week is the centre open?

c. What is the difference in price between the two sizes of slush puppies?

d. Which activity would you do first?

e. Write a bill and work out the total cost for the following:
bowling (2 adults, 2 kids), 4 soft drinks, 2 popcorn, 1 ice cream,
1 packet of crisps and 6 arcade games.

5. **Underline the true sentences. Rewrite them in your copybook.**

a. You can order lunch here. *false*

b. A child of 10 would pay €3 for bowling. *true*

c. It is open on Wednesdays from 4pm. *true*

d. It is not wheelchair-friendly. *false*

e. Nine-year olds can play darts. *false*

f. You could have a birthday party here. *true*

g. Bowling coaches are not available. *false*

h. 2 packets of crisps will cost €3. *true*

i. Ice-creams cost the same as popcorn. *true*

j. The centre is open 7 hours a day, Tuesday to Sunday. *false*

6. Write the missing letters.

| or | ar |

Use a dictionary to look up words you do not know.

| c___ ___pet | f___ ___k | t___ ___t | ___ ___chard |
| sh___ ___e | l___ ___k | d___ ___t | st___ ___m |

7. Write the missing letters (**or** or **ar**). Write out the full sentences.

a. This m___ ___ ning I worked on the farm.

_____

b. The m___ ___ket is a great place f___ ___ shopping.

_____

c. I wish you wouldn't sn___ ___e anym___ ___e.

_____

d. The th___ ___n is h___ ___d and sh___ ___p.

_____

e. The m___ ___rble flo___ ___ is slippery.

_____

8. Make words. Read the new words.

Add **ar**.
p___ ___t
sm___ ___t
p___ ___k
m___ ___lin
c___ ___t

Add **or**.
l___ ___d
b___ ___e
f___ ___m
st___ ___e
w___ ___n

Who is snoring?

9. Write six sentences in your copybook using some **or** and **ar** words. They can be silly. Example: The sh**ar**k w**or**e a st**ar** to the m**ar**ket.

Prepositions show the relationship between nouns or pronouns in a sentence.

> **Sample** The oranges are **on** my bed.

Other prepositions include: **below**, **between**, **until**, **around**, **in**, **above**.

Must I sit **in**, **on top**, **under** or **at** my desk?

10. Underline the prepositions in these sentences.
   a. Kelly could not get off the horse.
   b. I will work after I've had a rest.
   c. Place the ladder against the wall.
   d. She is going to dancing lessons.
   e. Read a book before you go to sleep.
   f. The ghost floated above my head.

11. Choose the correct preposition. Rewrite the sentences in your copybook.

last	by	beside	under	into	through	for	up

   a. I left your shoes _____ the door.
   b. Kevin wants to sit _____ Kelly.
   c. I did all my homework _____ night.
   d. My brother climbed _____ the tree.
   e. The bats flew _____ the cave.
   f. They escaped _____ the window.
   g. The dog was hiding _____ my bed.
   h. School will be closed _____ two weeks.

12. Make these words into sentences by adding prepositions.
   a. Nick is the table
   _____
   b. The goats went the bridge
   _____
   c. We danced the road
   _____
   d. There is a spider you
   _____
   e. Matt chased me the hill
   _____

Word list

medium	special	parties	adults	snacks	telephone
centre	ages	bowling	deposit	refreshments	opening

13. Learn the spellings. Now look and say, picture, cover, write, check.

_____   _____

_____   _____

_____   _____

_____   _____

_____   _____

14. Write any words you got wrong.

_____

15. Write the missing words. Use the word list.

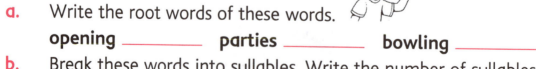

I will need a **deposit** please.

a. Another word for grown-ups is _____.

b. Phone is the short word for _____.

c. Emma has been to two birthday _____.

d. The disco is in the community _____.

e. I think the take-away is _____ at 4pm.

f. Children between the _____ of 8 and 12 should be doing chores.

16. Use these words to make sentences of your own.
    special, **medium**, **snacks**, **bowling**, **deposit** and **refreshments**.

17. Write the answers. Use the word list.

a. Write the root words of these words.
   opening _____ **parties** _____ **bowling** _____

b. Break these words into syllables. Write the number of syllables for each:
   telephone _____ **refreshments** _____ **special** _____

c. Write a word that is in plural form. _____

d. Write 1 word that has a **soft** c. _____

e. Underline the letter pattern that is the same in these words:
   bowling   opening

Talk about

18. Work with a friend. Demonstrate an activity that you enjoy. Your partner must guess what you are doing.

Write about

19. Design a flyer for a place you enjoy going to. Do a rough draft in your copybook. Check it, improve on it, then write it out neatly and add drawings.

> Tips for making a flyer:
> - Plan your layout and do a rough sketch first.
> - Include details such as: address, contact numbers, opening hours and cost.
> - The place name should be in bigger letters at the top or in the middle of the page. Smaller writing with the details should be at the bottom.
> - Your flyer should be eye-catching.
> - Say what is special about this place.
> - Include pictures.
> - Try to think of a catchy slogan.

> A score of 45 in darts is called a bag o' nuts.

> In snooker, soft contact between two balls is called a kiss.

Display your flyers in the classroom or make a class booklet.

20. Answer these quiz questions. You can colour one pin for each one you get right!

| a cue | 50 | billiards | 3 | 10 | 20 |
| bull's eye | strike | 7 | 1 | | |

a. What is the highest number on a dart board?
b. What is the very centre of a dart board called?
c. How many points is this worth?
d. How many darts do you throw in one turn?
e. How many pins are there in tenpin bowling?
f. What word means to knock down all the pins at once?
g. In snooker, how many points is the black ball worth?
h. What do you hit the snooker ball with?
i. How many white balls are there in snooker?
j. What is another name for the game of pool?

21. What was your score? _____

 Before you read... Do you know any heroes?

1. **Read the story.**

Hans, the hero of Haarlem

There is a country called the Netherlands where much of the land is lower than the level of the sea. This land does not flood because people have built great, thick walls called dykes. These dykes keep the sea out. They are there for the protection of the country and its people.

One day a boy called Hans and his brother Dieter went out to play. They went far away from their home where there were no houses, just green fields. They were playing by the dyke, when Dieter said, 'Hans, look at the little hole in the wall! Water is coming through!'

'What?' screamed Hans. He looked at the hole. 'Oh no! There's a hole in the dyke!' He looked all around, but there was not a person or house in sight. Hans knew the water would soon make a big gap in the dyke and the sea would come flooding in. But the town was so far away. If they ran to get help, it could be too late.

Suddenly Hans had an idea. He stuck his forefinger into the hole, and it fitted tightly. Then he said to his brother, 'Run and get help!'

Dieter ran off as fast as he could. Hans sat and waited. He waited and waited. His hand became cold and numb. Then the coldness crept up his arm and it began to ache. The pain spread to his neck. It felt like he had been sitting there for hours. Hans became frightened, but still he didn't move.

At last in the distance, he saw movement. It was the men from the town, including his father. They were running towards him with pickaxes and shovels. Hans felt great relief.

The men gave a great cheer when they saw Hans, who was now pale and shivering. They rubbed his aching arm.

Then the men set to work mending the dyke. Once it was done, they marched back to the town, carrying Hans high on their shoulders. He was a hero. To this day, the people tell the story of how a little boy saved the dyke.

> Mother Teresa was a heroine. She helped many people.

2. Talk about.

Do you think you are brave?
Talk about brave occupations.

3. Answer the questions.

a. Why were dykes built in the Netherlands?

_____

b. Who noticed the hole in the wall?

_____

c. Why was Hans worried?

_____

d. What did Hans do?

_____

e. How did Hans feel while sitting there?

_____

f. What did he see in the distance?

_____

g. Who came to help?

_____

4. Answer the questions in your copybook.

a. Why is the Netherlands in danger of flooding?
b. Were Hans and Dieter playing close to home?
   Support your answer with a quote.
   Do not forget quotation marks.
c. Why didn't both the boys run and get help?
d. How was Hans treated by his father and the men?
e. Do you think Hans was brave? Explain your answer.
f. What do you think you would have done?

5. In your copybook put the sentences in order.

Dieter ran to get help. Hans was a hero. Dieter and Hans were playing by the dyke. Their father and men from the town fixed the hole. Hans placed his finger in the hole. Dieter saw a hole in the wall.

6. Write the missing letters.

| er | ir | ur |

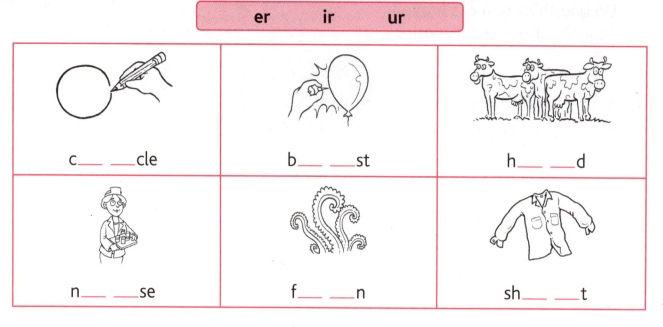

| c___ ___cle | b___ ___st | h___ ___d |
| n___ ___se | f___ ___n | sh___ ___t |

7. Complete the words using **er**, **ir** or **ur**. Write the sentences.

   a. She came th___ ___d in the sack race.

   _____

   b. I will sleep in on Sat___ ___day.

   _____

   c. A m___ ___maid will find it hard to walk.

   _____

   d. This t___ ___m I might come f___ ___st.

   _____

   e. That g___ ___l has a lot of en___ ___gy.

   _____

8. Make words. Read the new words.

   Add **er**.   Add **ir**.   Add **ur**.
   h___ ___   d___ ___ty   b___ ___n
   s___ ___ve   s___ ___   c___ ___ly
   w___ ___e   th___ ___ty   t___ ___key
   st___ ___n   f___ ___m   h___ ___l
   ev___ ___y   sk___ ___t   f___ ___nish
   m___ ___cy   m___ ___ror   c___ ___tain

That bird is absurd.

9. Write six sentences in your copybook using **er**, **ir** and **ur** words.
   They can be silly! Example: The nurse gave a girl a gherkin first.

Plural means more than one.

> **Sample** book – books, match – matches, fairy – fairies

10. Write the words in plural form.

a. worry _____
b. knife _____
c. yourself _____
d. pillow _____
e. school _____
f. flash ___es___
g. bicycle ___s___

h. watch ___es___
i. berry ___ies___
j. curry ___ies___
k. dish ___es___
l. donkey ___s___
m. kidney ___s___
n. diary ___ies___

If a word ends in **o** then add **s** or **es**.

> **Sample** tomato – tomatoes, cello – cellos

11. Write the words in plural form.

a. tornado ___es___
b. rodeo ___s___
c. video ___s___
d. banjo ___es___
e. tomato ___es___
f. disco ___s___
g. kangaroo ___s___

h. piano ___s___
i. volcano ___es___
j. potato ___es___
k. photo ___s___
l. cuckoo ___s___
m. mango ___s___
n. domino ___es___

Sometimes words can change completely in plural form, and sometimes not at all.

> **Sample** mouse – mice; fish – fish.

The monkeys enjoyed the berries.

12. Write these words in plural form.

a. child ___ren___
b. ox ___es___
c. trout ___et___
d. foot ___2 feet___
e. sheep _____
f. salmon ___s___
g. octopus ___ii___

h. deer _____
i. goose ___ee___
j. woman ___women___
k. cactus ___ii___
l. tooth ___teeth___
m. moose _____
n. doorman ___doormen___

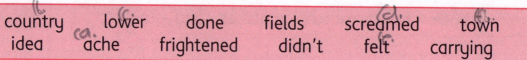
Word list

country	lower	done	fields	screamed	town
idea	ache	frightened	didn't	felt	carrying

13. Learn the spellings. Now look and say, picture, cover, write, check.

_____   _____

_____   _____

_____   _____

_____   _____

14. Write any words you got wrong.

_____

15. Write the missing words. Use the word list.

a. With all this work my hand will _____.

b. The beautiful _____ I live in is Ireland.

c. Look on the _____ shelf for the teabags.

d. My sister _____ when she saw a beetle.

e. I _____ sick after eating the whole chocolate cake.

f. The next _____ is six miles away.

16. In your copybook use these words to make sentences of your own:
done, fields, idea, frightened, didn't and **carrying**.

I didn't do it!

17. Write the answers. Use the word list.

a. Write the root words for these.

frightened _____ **screamed** _____

carrying _____ **lower** _____

b. Write the words that end with these:

try _____ **own** _____ **he** _____ **one** _____

c. Break these words into syllables. Write the number of syllables for each.

country _____ **idea** _____

d. Write this word in full. **didn't** _____

e. Write the words that have an **ea** pattern. _____

f. Write a word where **ch** has a **k** sound. _____

Talk about

18. Work with a group. Act out the story of *Hans, the hero of Haarlem*. It should include a person from the town giving a speech about the bravery of Hans.

Write about

19. Write the same story for younger children. Remember to keep it simple. Do your rough work in your copybook.

> Tips for writing for younger readers:
> - The words should be simple.
> - Do not have too much detail in the sentences.
> - The print should be bigger.
> - Add lots of pictures.

> A hero is someone who shows great bravery or is a champion.

Once you are happy with your story, write it out neatly in your copybook and add a picture. Put all the stories together for the Infant classes.

20. Work out the coded saying.

A	B	C	D	E	F	G	H	I	J	K	L	M
#	■	%	➤	✳	±	◆	▲	❀	●	❑	★	☆
N	O	P	Q	R	S	T	U	V	W	X	Y	Z
❖	☺	○	▼	◗	✷	❖	☆	◇	✪	♥	♠	⊥

▲✳◗☺ ☺❖★♠ #○✳#◗✷ ✪▲▲✳❖ ❖▲★ ❖✷◆✳◗ ❀✷ ➤✳#➤

A Hero only Appears when the Tiger is dead.

21. Use the codes to write the names of some heroes you know or have heard about.

_____

_____

_____

What is an earthquake?

1. Read the text.

The San Francisco earthquake

It was early in the morning of Wednesday the 18th April, 1906. Most people were asleep. Then suddenly everything changed. At 5.13am, the earth beneath San Francisco shook. It shook for forty seconds. Then there was ten seconds of calm, followed by another shock and a loud, rumbling roar from the ground.

Everywhere was confusion. People came rushing into the streets, grabbing whatever they could. Glass and windows shattered, buildings came tumbling down, roads buckled and clouds of dust filled the air. Whole areas of the city collapsed or sank into the ground. People looked at their city in horror.

Five hours after the first tremor, a fire broke out. It spread quickly. Fire-fighters rushed to put out the blaze, but there was no water. The earthquake had damaged the water pipes. The city went up in flames and the fire department was helpless to stop it. Thousands of people had escaped the city and they watched from the hills as large areas of their city burned down.

Fierce winds caused the fires to go on for three days. At last it began to rain. Smoke rose from the smouldering ruins. There was nothing left of block after block of houses. The few buildings left standing were just empty shells. The old San Francisco was gone forever.

Shocking facts
- The earthquake lasted 65 seconds
- It caused 700 deaths.
- 28,000 buildings were destroyed.
- 300,000 people were left homeless.
- Two-thirds of the city was wiped out.
- The city shook because it lies on the San Andreas Fault which is a big gash in the Earth's surface. An earthquake deep underground ripped the fault apart.

I saw chunks of plaster fall from the walls.

I was awakened by a very severe shock. The shaking was so violent it nearly threw me out of bed.

2. **Talk about.**

   If you had to grab something precious in a hurry, what would it be? Talk about natural disasters.

3. **Answer the questions.**

   a. When did the earthquake happen?

       _____

   b. Where did it occur?

       _____

   c. For how long did it last?

       _____

   d. What were most people doing when the earthquake occurred?

       _____

   e. What broke out five hours after the earthquake?

       _____

   f. Why was there no water?

       _____

   g. Why did the wind make the situation worse?

       _____

   h. What eventually put out the fire?

       _____

4. **Answer the questions in your copybook.**

   a. Write two sentences to describe the scene.
   b. How did the people feel? Support your answer with quotes.
   c. How did the disaster affect the people of San Francisco?
   d. What is the San Andreas Fault?
   e. What do you think would be the most frightening part of an earthquake?

5. **Find words in the story with the same meaning. Use a dictionary.**

   a. broke into pieces   _____
   b. fell down   _____
   c. ruined   _____
   d. unable to help   _____
   e. strong (winds)   _____
   f. without a home   _____

6. Write the missing letters.

or	ar	er

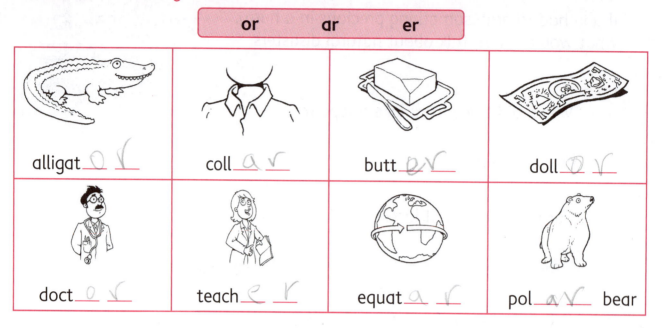

alligat**or** ✓	coll**ar** ✓	butt**er** ✓	doll**ar** ✓
doct**or** ✓	teach**er** ✓	equat**ar** ✓	pol**ar** ✓ bear

7. Complete the words using **or**, **ar** or **er**. Write the sentences.

a. I will mark the date on my calend___ ___.

_____

b. Put on your indicat___ ___ if you turn.

_____

c. The burgl___ ___ stole my slipp___ ___.

_____

d. My broth___ ___ has a caterpill___ ___.

_____

e. I felt terr**ar** ✓ going into the cell**er** ✓.

_____

8. Make words. Read the new words.

Add **er**.	Add **ar**.	Add **or**.
lett___ ___	begg___ ___	err___ ___
lobst___ ___	sol___ ___	horr___ ___
fath___ ___	regul___ ___	decorat___ ___
moth___ ___	lun___ ___	radiat___ ___
digg___ ___	pill___ ___	operat___ ___
jogg___ ___	rad___ ___	surviv___ ___

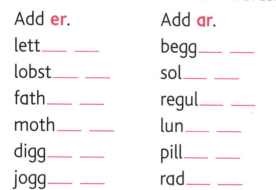

The burgl**ar** stole my alligat**or**.

9. In your copybook write six sentences using words with **ar**, **or** or **er** endings. They can be silly! Example: My fath**er** is a bett**er** act**or** than the lobst**er**.

10. Rewrite these sentences in your copybook.
    Add capital letters, commas, full stops and exclamation marks.

There's a spider on your head!

   a. on my plate i have peas mash carrots meat and gravy
   b. get off my lawn immediately
   c. brad and jackie are going to niamh's party in march
   d. my brother sam wants mexican food for his christmas dinner
   e. tim can dance sing and smile at the same time
   f. ben's parents have been to italy greece france and sweden
   g. be careful of the piranhas in that river
   h. in her lunchbox jill has bread yoghurt an apple and a worm

11. Write the correct prepositions.

above	between	around	on	along	until

   a. Put the ham _____ the two slices of bread.
   b. That is a halo _____ your head.
   c. We are at school _____ 3pm.
   d. They walked _____ the stream.
   e. The shop is _____ the corner.
   f. There is chewing gum _____ your shoe.

12. Write the sentences in plural form.
   a. The (fisherman) caught many (fish).

       _____

   b. The (ferry) crossed the (sea).

       _____

   c. We could hear the (echo) of the crowd at the (match).

       _____

   d. The (wife) of the (king) posed for the (photo).

       _____

   e. The (horse), (donkey), (goose) and (sheep) lived on the farm.

       _____

   f. There are many (fly) around the (bunch) of bananas.

       _____

   g. The (eye-witness) helped the (policeman).

       _____

   h. The (fox) ate my (lolly)!

       _____

Word list

early	suddenly	earth	beneath	loud	everywhere
whatever	buildings	clouds	areas	earthquake	large	forever

13. Learn the spellings. Now look and say, picture, cover, write, check.

_____   _____
_____   _____
_____   _____
_____   _____
_____   _____
_____   _____
_____

14. Write any words you got wrong.

_____

15. Write the missing words. Use the word list.

a.   _____ you do, do not touch that rhino.
b.   We live on a planet called _____.
c.   Desmond said he would love me _____.
d.   Do not play in the muddy _____
      of the playground.
e.   The _____ bird catches the worm.
f.   I looked _____ for my Maths book.
g.   The _____ in our town date back to the 1800s.

> Clean your room, do your homework, feed the bird!

> Whatever!

16. In your copybook use these words to make sentences of your own:
    suddenly, **beneath**, **loud**, **clouds**, **earthquake** and **large**.

17. Write the answers. Use the word list.

a.   Write four compound words and circle the two smaller words in each.
      (Remember: A compound word is made up of two words.)

      _____

b.   Write words that have an **ea** pattern. _____
      Do they sound the same? _____

c.   Break these words into syllables. Write the number of syllables for
      each.   **suddenly** _____   **buildings** _____

d.   Write a word that has a **soft g**. _____

e.   Underline the letter pattern that is the same in these words.
      loud   **clouds**

Talk about

18. Work with a friend. Act out an interview between a reporter and a survivor of the earthquake. Swap roles.

Write about

19. Imagine you were a survivor of the San Francisco earthquake. In your copybook write your diary entry for that day. Write your rough draft here.

Dear Diary,

_____

_____

_____

_____

_____

_____

_____

_____

> The San Andreas Fault runs for 600 miles.

20. Work out the levels of the Richter Scale.
    1. Add **al** to **instrument**. _____
    2. Change **b** in **beetle** to a **f**, change **t** to **b**. _____
    3. Change **fr** to **sl** in **fright**. _____
    4. Change **w** in **mower** to a **d** and add **ate**. _____
    5. Change **i** in **string** to an **o**. RATHER _____
    6. Change **w** in **wrong** to **st**. _____
    7. Change **b** in **berry** to **v** and drop an **r**. _____ STRONG
    8. Add **ive** to **destruct**. _____
    9. Change **a** in **rain** to **u** and add **ous**. _____
    10. Add **ous** to **disaster** and remove the **e**. _____
    11. Change the **f** in **fern** to **v** and change the **n** to **y**. _____ DISASTROUS.
    12. Add **astrophic** to **cat**. _____

What stories do you know that feature witches?

1. Read the poem.

Two witches discuss good grooming

'How do you keep your teeth so green
Whilst mine remain so white?
Although I rub them vigorously
With cold slime every night.'

'Your eyes are such a lovely shade
Of bloodshot, streaked with puce.
I prod mine daily with a stick
But it isn't any use.'

'I envy so, the spots and boils
That brighten your complexion.
Even rat spit on my face
Left no trace of infection.'

'I've even failed to have bad breath
After eating sewage raw,
Yet your halitosis
Can strip paint from a door.'

'My dear, there is no secret,
Now I don't mean to brag.
What you see is nature's work
I'm just a natural hag.'

John Coldwell

Luna Lovegood is a witch in a
Harry Potter book.

2. Talk about.

What do you think a witch looks like?

3. Answer the questions.

a. Who is talking in the poem?

_____

b. What does she do to her teeth?

_____

c. Describe the second witch's eyes.

_____

d. What had the witch put on her skin?

_____

e. What is the title of the poem?

_____

f. Who wrote the poem?

_____

4. Find quotes from the poem to match these sentences. Do not forget the quotation marks.

a. The witch rubs her teeth hard.

_____

b. She prods her eyes every day.

_____

c. She is jealous of the other witch's spots.

_____

d. The other witch has bad breath.

_____

e. The witch put saliva on her face.

_____

f. Do you think the witch who speaks first is a real witch? Explain your answer.

_____

5. What do these words mean? Use a dictionary.

a. remain _____   c. prod _____

b. halitosis _____   d. hag _____

6. In your copybook draw and label one of the witches. Get your clues from the poem.

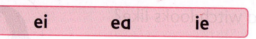
7. Write the missing letters. Write out the full sentences.

ei	ea	ie

a. Did you get a rec ___ ___ pt when you bought that?

_____

b. The crop did y ___ ___ ld a good harvest.

_____

c. Mind the st ___ ___ m from the kettle.

_____

d. You should never l ___ ___ .

_____

e. I like gravy on my st ___ ___ k.

_____

8. Write the missing letters. Write out the full sentences.

ey	ow	ai

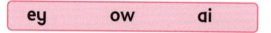

The donkey will **mow** the lawn.

a. The monk _e_ _y_ snatched the bananas.

_____

b. I seem to be sl _o_ _w_ in the mornings.

_____

c. Will this r _a_ _i_ n ever stop?

_____

d. You should smile and not fr _o_ _w_ n.

_____

e. The owl swooped on its pr _e_ _y_ .

_____

9. Write the missing letters. Write out the full sentences.

ar	or	ir	ur	er

a. The rabbit's f _u_ _r_ was very soft.

_____

b. My sist _e_ _r_ is as good as gold.

_____

c. P _a_ _r_ k your bike by the gate.

_____

d. The tract _o_ _r_ was very old.

_____

e. Do not get d _i_ _r_ ty before dinner.

_____

Nouns are naming words.
Proper nouns are specific names for people, pets and places. (Larry, Cork, Paris)
Common nouns are general names for things. (chair, book, bird)
Collective nouns are groups of things. (a bunch of flowers, a flock of sheep)

10. Use suitable nouns to complete the sentences.
    Rewrite the sentences in your copybook.

    a. The silly _____ ran across the _____.
    b. The _____ was bitten by a vicious _____.
    c. The _____ went up to the _____.
    d. The _____ kissed the _____.
    e. The _____ was chasing the _____.
    f. I have a sore _____ so I will go to the _____.

11. Complete the collective nouns.

> parliament   pod   gaggle   swarm   cast   clutch
> leap   flight   shoal   herd   chorus   nest   pride   troop

    a. a _____ of geese
    b. a _____ of stairs
    c. a _____ of cattle
    d. a _____ of mice
    e. a _____ of actors
    f. a _____ of seals
    g. a _____ of monkeys
    h. a _____ of bees
    i. a _____ of leopards
    j. a _____ of lions
    k. a _____ of angels
    l. a _____ of eggs
    m. a _____ of owls
    n. a _____ of fish

12. Write three nouns for each group.

school objects			
vegetables			
wild animals			
surnames			
cities			
dairy products			
flowers			
shops			

Word list

teeth	mine	shade	daily	isn't	envy	brighten
just	failed	breath	secret	natural	discuss	

13. Learn the spellings. Now look and say, picture, cover, write, check.

_____   _____

_____   _____

_____   _____

_____   _____

_____   _____

14. Write any words you got wrong.

_____

15. Write the missing words. Use the word list.

   a. You _____ the test because you did not learn.

   b. I tidy my room _____ .

   c. I know the largest present is _____ .

   d. This healthy bar is made from _____ ingredients.

   e. The teacher will _____ the project with the class.

   f. Brush your _____ twice a day.

   g. My friends will _____ my delicious lunch.

16. In your copybook use these words to make sentences of your own:
isn't, **secret**, **shade**, **brighten**, **just** and **breath**.

*I need some **shade**!*

17. Write the answers. Use the word list.

   a. Write the word **isn't** in full. _____

   b. Find smaller words in these words from the list:
mine _____ **shade** _____ **breath** _____

   c. Count the number of syllables in each word:
daily _____ **natural** _____ **brighten** _____

   d. Write a word that has a **silent e.** _____

   e. Underline the letter pattern that is the same in these words.
failed   daily

   f. Write the root words of these words:
brighten _____ **natural** _____ **failed** _____

Talk about

18. Work with a group. Recite the poem
Two witches discuss good grooming. Use expression!

Write about

19. In your copybook write a spell poem using ten ingredients. Each ingredient needs an adjective to describe it (for example, slimy fish eyes, warty frogs). Do not forget to say what your spell is for. Look at this example.

Spell to turn teachers into turtles

Slimy fish eyes,
warty frogs,
beetle eggs, and
hairs of dogs.

20. Follow the instructions to draw a witch.

Sabrina the teenage witch is a popular TV series.

Before you read...

Do you have a pet at home?

1. Read the pet column.

PET COLUMN

FOR SALE: Jack Russell pups, small breed, brown and white, pedigree, inoculated, dewormed, 12 weeks old, phone: 5556743

WANTED: good homes for beautiful fluffy kittens, 8 weeks old, phone: 5553421

Pooch Parlour

Grooming service

Appointment only
Call Martin 5553212

Don't lose your pet!
Have your dog or cat microchipped today. Painless and quick service. Call 5553422 for more information.

Ballywater Dog Home
Stripes is looking for a loving home. He is good with children and enjoys playing ball. He will benefit from a family who will have time to play with him. Neutered, inoculated and dewormed. Call 5556789

FOR SALE: Red setter pups, call 5554322

PETS PARADISE:
Stockists of quality pet food, pet toys, pet accessories. Advice on pet care available.
Monthly specials.
14 Main Street
Phone: 5552674

WANTED: Good home for a 5-year old black and white spayed female cat. Owner moving country. She is an affectionate and loyal pet who needs a calm and loving environment. Call 55532123

TICKET SELLERS needed to sell raffle tickets, great prizes, all proceeds to I.S.P.C.A. Please support this worthy cause. Call 5554636

PERFECT PAWS
- Boarding house for cats and dogs.
- Personal attention
- Large runs
- Clean and safe
- Daily walks
- Toys

Home away from home
Phone: 55534333

Sir Isaac Newton, a noted cat lover, invented the cat flap.

Dogs were probably domesticated from wolves 15,000 years ago.

2. Talk about.

What things should you do for your pet every day?

3. Answer the questions.

a. Where is *Pets Paradise*?

_____

b. How old are the Jack Russell puppies?

_____

c. Name a boarding house for pets.

_____

d. What number would you call for Red Setter puppies?

_____

e. What does the I.S.P.C.A. want you to do?

_____

f. Why does the black and white cat need a home?

_____

4. Complete the sentences.

a. You need to make an _____ at the *Pooch Parlour*.

b. *Perfect Paws* will give your dogs _____ walks.

c. The _____ kittens are 8 weeks old.

d. Have your pet _____ to avoid losing it.

e. *Pets Paradise* will give you _____ on pet care.

f. Stripes needs a _____ family.

5. Write the sentences that are true. There are three.

The boarding house will look after your hamster.
Pets Paradise has weekly specials.
The Jack Russell pups are brown and white.
Being micro-chipped is not painful for animals.
Stripes will be better off with a family that has children.
The five-year old cat needs a busy and noisy home.

_____

_____

_____

6. In your copybook describe a pet you would like to have. Give reasons for your choice.

ar often says **or** after **w**.

| Sample war |

or often says **er** after **w**.

| Sample worker |

7.   Write the missing letters.

| **ar**   **or** |

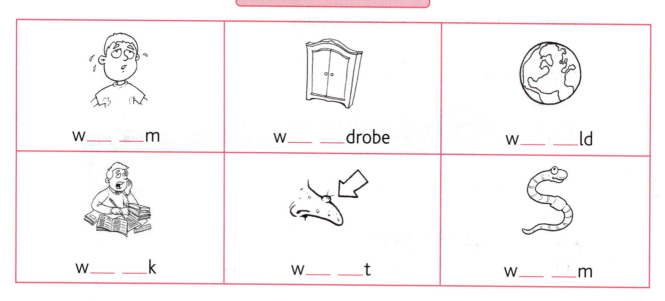

| w___ ___m | w___ ___drobe | w___ ___ld |
| w___ ___k | w___ ___t | w___ ___m |

8.   Complete the words using **ar** or **or**. Write the sentences.

a.   That was the w___ ___st test I have done.

_____

b.   The bird w___ ___bles in the early morning.

_____

c.   The nurse visits the w___ ___d at nine.

_____

d.   Glenda is a hard w___ ___ker.

_____

e.   You have had your last w___ ___ning.

_____

9.   Make words. Read the new words.

Add **wor**.   Add **war**.

___ ___ ___th   ___ ___ ___p
___ ___ ___se   d___ ___ ___f
___ ___ ___d   ___ ___ ___den

Are you **wor**king hard?

10. Write six sentences in your copybook using **war** and **wor** words. They can be silly! Example: The w**or**m goes to w**or**k in the w**ar**drobe.

Verbs are action words.

> **Sample** I **ran** around the field. I **am** hot.

Remember: Some verbs need a helping verb.

> **Sample** I **have done** all my work already.

11. Underline the verbs and helping words in this paragraph.

The loudest things in the ocean are shrimps. The blue whale produces the loudest noise of an individual animal in the sea, but the loudest natural noise is made by trillions of shrimps. The noise is caused by the shrimps snapping their single claws. The noise comes from burst bubbles. The sound of the *shrimp layer* amounts to about 160 decibels in the air; much louder than a jet taking off. Some have compared it to everyone in the world frying bacon at the same time. Shrimps use this noise to stun prey, communicate and find mates.

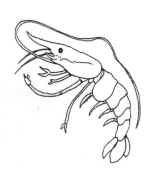

12. Use suitable verbs to complete these sentences. Make sure you use the right form of the verb. Read your sentences to make sure they sound right.

a. The cows _____ happily in the field.

b. My brother _____ over the fence.

c. I _____ choc-chip muffins.

d. The children _____ during lunch break.

e. The postman _____ our letters to the door.

f. My Dad often _____ in the living room.

Adverbs tell us more about the verb

> **Sample** He spoke **loudly**.

To change an adjective into an adverb we often add **ly**.

> **Sample** slow**ly**

13. Change the words in brackets into adverbs.

a. The sun shone (brilliant) over the playground. _____

b. The child coughed (polite). _____

c. Line up (quick) and (quiet). _____

d. We stood (patient) in the queue. _____

e. The teacher spoke (calm) and (clear). _____

Word list

fluffy	beautiful	service	lose	loving	advice	female
perfect	painless	monthly	loyal	prizes	support	ticket

14. Learn the spellings. Now look and say, picture, cover, write, check.

_____   _____
_____   _____
_____   _____
_____   _____
_____   _____
_____   _____

15. Write any words you got wrong.

_____

16. Fill in the missing words. Use the word list.

> **Support** your local library!

   a. There will be _____ at the raffle.

   b. Ned pays his bills _____.

   c. Show your _____ to the bus conductor.

   d. Take my _____ and work hard at school.

   e. _____ a charity of your choice.

   f. The opposite of male is _____.

   g. Having an injection is _____.

17. In your copybook use these words to make sentences of your own:
fluffy, **beautiful**, **service**, **lose**, **loving**, **perfect** and **loyal**.

18. Write the answers. Use the word list.

   a. Write the root words of these words from the list.
      beautiful _____   **loving** _____
      painless _____   **monthly** _____

   b. Find a word from the list that has a **soft** c. _____

   c. Write a mnemonic that helps you to spell **beautiful**.

      _____

   d. Count the number of syllables in each word.
      fluffy _____ **perfect** _____ **female** _____ **support** _____

   e. Write two words that have a **silent e.**

      _____

Talk about

19. Work with a friend. Have a conversation between a pet and its owner. Swap roles.

Write about

20. You are looking for a pet so you place an advert in the pet column. Do not forget to add your contact details. Show your advert to your friend.

PET COLUMN

According to folklore, if a cat sleeps with all four paws tucked under its body, it is a sign that cold weather is on the way.

21. Write the dog breeds in the word ladder. The next word must start with the last letter of the previous word.

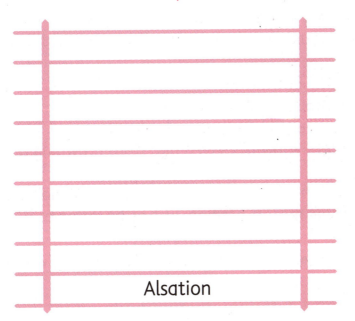

Alsation

Longdog
Rough Collie
Thai Ridgeback
King Charles Spaniel
German Coolies
Norwich Terrier
Spanish Mastiff
Feist
English Cocker Spaniel

Before you read...

Do you keep your word?

I. **Read the story.**

The five-coloured deer (a Japanese folk tale)

A very long time ago, a very rare deer lived in the forest. It was a special deer with white horns and a five-coloured coat. No-one even knew it existed.

One day a weary traveller fell into the river by the forest. He cried out for help. Only the deer heard him. The deer took pity on the man. The noble deer stretched out its horns for the man to grasp. The man was pulled to safety.

'Thank you for saving my life,' said the man. 'How can I ever repay you?'

The deer said, 'My coat is very valuable because it is so rare. I have to hide myself in the forest, away from greedy hunters. You must promise never to tell anyone about my secret hiding-place.'

The man said, 'I will not breathe a word to anyone. That is a promise. Thank you and goodbye.'

Sometime later the queen of the land had a dream. She dreamt of a five-coloured deer with white horns. She wanted to own this animal. The king offered a reward to anyone who could bring this animal to the queen.

The man who had been saved by the deer brought the king and his men to the forest. He promised them he would find the creature. Soon they did find it and the deer was surrounded.

The deer asked the king, 'Who told you of my hiding-place?'
'This noble man here,' said the king. 'He will receive a large reward.'
'This man is not noble, sir,' said the deer. 'I saved him from drowning and he has betrayed me.'
'Oh! That changes things,' said the king to the deer. 'You are the noble one. Now you will go free and he will receive nothing, just as he deserves.'

From that time on deer were never hunted. The five-coloured deer was safe.

2. Talk about.

Why is it important to keep a promise?

3. Answer the questions.

a. Why was the deer special?

_____

b. What happened to the weary traveller?

_____

c. What promise did the man make?

_____

d. What dream did the queen have?

_____

e. What is the moral of the story?

_____

f. Where does this story come from?

_____

4. Complete the sentences.

a. The deer had white horns and a _____ coat.

b. He had a _____ hiding place.

c. The deer _____ the man's life.

d. The king offered a reward of _____.

e. The deer said the _____ had betrayed him.

f. The king let the _____ go free.

g. From then on deer were never _____ again.

5. In your copybook write these sentences in order.

The man told the king where the deer could be found. The deer was safe. The man received nothing. It saved a man from drowning. The rare deer lived in the forest.

6. Answer the questions in your copybook.

a. Do you think the deer was kind? Say why/why not.

b. What kind of character do you think the man had?

c. Do you think the story has a good ending? Give reasons for your answer.

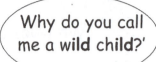

7. Write the missing letter patterns.

ild	ind	int

a. I am a good ch___ ___ ___ .
b. A bat is not bl___ ___ ___.
c. I have a t___ ___ ___ of blue in my hair.
d. Do not eat the r___ ___ ___ of the lemon.
e. A m___ ___ ___ will make your breath fresh.

'Why do you call me a **wild** child?'

8. Write the missing letter patterns.

olt	old	ost

a. I s___ ___ ___ my bicycle for €30.
b. The c___ ___ ___ ran around the paddock.
c. The teacher l___ ___ ___ our books.
d. The b___ ___ ___ class stayed in at break.
e. Our h___ ___ ___ offered us tea.

9. Change the word families but make sure the words still make sense.

Example w**ild** – w**ind**

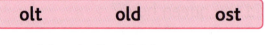

ind	ost	old

m**ild** - _____   b**olt** - _____   h**ind** - _____

p**int** - _____   c**ost** - _____   f**old** - _____

10. Write three words for each letter pattern.

a. ent – tent   _____   _____   _____
b. ink – think   _____   _____   _____
c. ack – snack   _____   _____   _____
d. ump – thump   _____   _____   _____
e. ook – shook   _____   _____   _____

11. Write six sentences in your copybook using words with letter patterns from this page.

Adjectives describe nouns.

> **Sample** **fluffy** slippers.

My work is **neat**, **perfect** and **correct**.

12. Write two adjectives to describe each word.

a. _____, _____ bird
b. _____, _____ friend
c. _____, _____ cake
d. _____, _____ shirt
e. _____, _____ day
f. _____, _____ game
g. _____, _____ chair
h. _____, _____ garden

13. Add adjectives to expand the sentences. Write the sentences in your copybook.

a. The man drove a car.
b The dog played in the garden.
c. The boy read a book.
d. The class ate burgers.
e. The teacher sat on her chair.

When we compare adjectives, we use the comparative and superlative form of the word.

> **Sample** cheap – cheaper – cheapest

If the word ends in a **y** change the **y** to an **i** before adding **er** and **est**.

> **Sample** happy – happier – happiest

14. Write the comparative and superlative forms.

a. easy _____
b. sunny _____
c. windy _____
d. scary _____
e. noisy _____
f. grumpy _____
g. silky _____
h. silly _____
i. pretty _____
j. lazy _____

Word list

rare	forest	no-one	cried	coat	promise	reward
diamonds	receive	drowning	changes	deserves	word	pity

15. Learn the spellings. Now look and say, picture, cover, write, check.

_____   _____
_____   _____
_____   _____
_____   _____
_____   _____
_____   _____

16. Write any words you got wrong.

_____

17. Write the missing words. Use the word list.

   a. The crown was encrusted with _____.
   b. My rabbit has a soft, white _____.
   c. It is such a _____ we can't play the match.
   d. Always keep a _____.
   e. To prevent _____ be very careful in water.
   f. The teacher made _____ to our timetable.
   g. _____ has completed their work yet.

18. Use these words to make sentences of your own.
    rare, **forest**, **cried**, **reward**, **receive**, **deserves** and **word**.

   *Your room is tidy. That is **rare**.*

19. Write the answers. Use the word list.

   a. Write a word from the list that has a **soft g**. _____
   b. Write a word from the list that has **soft c**. _____
   c. Find smaller words in these words from the list: **rare** _____
      forest _____ **reward** _____ **word** _____ **pity** _____
   d. Count the number of syllables in each word.
      reward _____ **promise** _____ **diamonds** _____
   e. Write the root words of these words:
      cried _____ **changes** _____ **drowning** _____
   f. Underline the letter pattern that is the same in these words:
      forest   word

Talk about

20. Work with a group. Act out the story of *The five-coloured deer*.

Write about

21. In your copybook tell the story in your own words. Write sentences for each picture.

Tips for writing a story in your own words:
- Give the story a different title.
- Your story should have a beginning, a middle and an end.
- Use describing words to make your story more interesting.
- Always read through your work when you have finished.
- Correct any mistakes and try to improve on it.

Male deer are called stags, females are does and babies are called fawns.

22. Work out the message by finding the letters.

My 1st is in star but not in rots. ___
My 2nd is in slim but not in miss. ___
My 3rd is in raw but not in car. ___
My 4th is in pain but not in pine. ___
My 5th is in tray but not in arts. ___
My 6th is in sport but not in troop. ___

My 1st is in desk but not in sped. ___
My 2nd is in read but not in dark. ___
My 3rd is in lime but not in milk. ___
My 4th is in spot but not in toes. ___

My 1st is in yard but not in dart. ___
My 2nd is in stone but not in nests. ___
My 3rd is in tube but not in best. ___
My 4th is in tram but not in mats. ___

My 1st is in wind but not in dine. ___
My 2nd is in one but not in ten. ___
My 3rd is in robe but not in bone. ___
My 4th is in card but not in race. ___

23. Write out the message here.

_____

_____

 Before you read...

What birds do you have in your neighbourhood?

1. Read the text.

Owls

Most owls are nocturnal birds. This means they hunt at night. They roost during the day, often in holes inside tree trunks.

Ireland has two types of owls, the long-eared owl and the barn owl. The barn owl is found in every continent except Antarctica.

Small owls eat mostly insects. Bigger owls eat mice and shrews. Eagle owls can even catch young deer!

Owls have eyes that face forwards. They cannot move their eyes and they swivel their whole head to look to the side or back. Their eyes are huge and they can see well in the dark.

To help keep their movements quiet, owls have fringed and soft edges on their wing feathers. They also have feathers on their legs and feet. All these features mean that owls can swoop down almost silently on their prey.

Owls have ears on the sides of their heads that are hidden by feathers. They can hear four times better than a cat. The 'ear-tufts' have nothing to do with hearing.

The number of owls in Ireland is decreasing. There are a few things you can do to help owls.

- Leave owl-nesting sites alone. These can often be found in old out-buildings or barns.
- Make sure that any owl-nesting sites are dry and have shelter.
- Leave old hollow trees where owls may be roosting. You can put out special nesting boxes for barn owls.

> Someone who studies birds is called an ornithologist.

2. **Talk about.**

How can we attract birds to our gardens?

3. **Answer the questions.**

a.   Where do owls often roost?

_____

b.   Which owls are found in Ireland?

_____

c.   What do owls eat?

_____

d.   How do owls look to the side?

_____

e.   Can you see an owl's ears? Explain your answer.

_____

f.   Where can owl nesting sites be found?

_____

g.   Name one thing you can do to help owls.

_____

4. **Complete the sentences.**

a.   Owls ____sleep____ during the day and ____hunt____ at night.

b.   The ____owl____ is found on almost every continent.

c.   Owls have ____fringe____ on their wing feathers.

d.   The ear tufts do not help the owl to ____hear____.

e.   The ____number____ of owls in Ireland is going down.

f.   You should not ____harm____ owl nesting sites.

g.   Owl nesting sites should be kept ____safe____.

5. **Answer these questions in your copybook.**

a.   How do you think the barn owl got its name?

b.   Do you think owls are better hunters than cats? Give a reason for your answer.

c.   Find words in the story with the same meaning as these:

active at night _____   perch or settle for sleep _____

turn around _____   very quietly _____

ch can make different sounds.

> **Sample** **ch** as in **chair**, or a **k** sound as in **chemist**, or a **sh** sound as in **chef**.

6. Complete the words where **ch** makes a **k** sound.

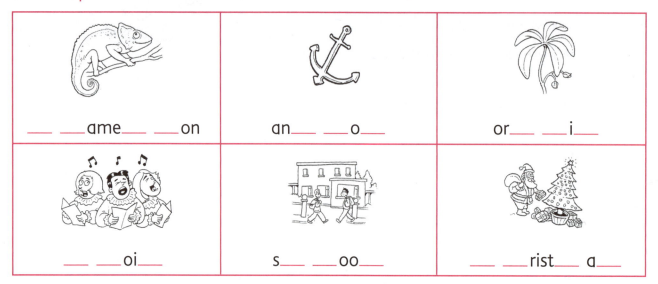

__ __ame__ __on	an__ __o__	or__ __i__
__ __oi__	s__ __oo__	__ __rist__ a__

7. Complete the words where **ch** makes a **sh** sound.

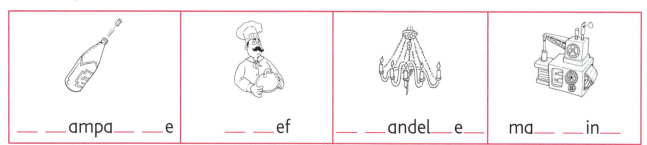

__ __ampa__ __e	__ __ef	__ __andel__e__	ma__ __in__

8. The letters **ch** can make different sounds. Sort the words by their sound.

> chic   chord   chess   ache   Chicago   chase   watch   echo   charade

ch as in chair	**ch** as in chef	**ch** as in chemist

9. Write six sentences in your copybook using some **ch** words. They can be silly!
    Example: The **ch**amelion had **ch**ampagne for **Ch**ristmas.

Pronouns take the place of nouns.

Sample Mandy asked some tortoises to tea. **She** gave **them** tea and cake.

Examples of pronouns: she, he, we, I, you, us, they, it, who, her

10. Fill in the pronouns to complete the sentences.

    a. Kim loves ice-cream. _____ ate a whole tub.

    b. Michele and I were talking. _____ have to sit apart now.

    c. The children were snoring. _____ were tired.

    d. The school is cold. _____ has no heating.

    e. Pauline took Freddie for a walk. _____ had to drag _____ along.

    f. Is that the teacher _____ plays football?

    g. He is almost as clever as _____ am.

    h. My work is neat but _____ is untidy.

We love teddies.

Do not use **them** incorrectly,
e.g. *Get me them books*. It should be,
Get me those books.

11. Look at the underlined pronouns.
Write the person or object that the pronoun stands for.

    a. 'I don't like pizza,' said Ron to Mick. _____

    b. 'Did you see the U.F.O.?' James asked Lilly. _____

    c. I love this music. It relaxes me. _____

    d. Stan heard his dog barking so he went to investigate. _____

    e. Roisin helped me with my project. She is so helpful. _____

12. Write your own sentences using these pronouns.

    a. her - _____

    b. our - _____

    c. my - _____

    d. you - _____

    e. us - _____

Word list

owls	nocturnal	during	except	insects	eagle	shelter
movements	quiet	prey	sites	edges	silently	hidden	trunks

13. Learn the spellings. Now look and say, picture, cover, write, check.

_____   _____
_____   _____
_____   _____
_____   _____
_____   _____
_____   _____
_____

14. Write any words you got wrong.

_____

15. Write the missing words. Use the word list.

a. The class should be working _____.

b. Beetles, flies and moths are all _____.

c. Leah has _____ her plate under her bed.

d. The _____ is a bird of prey.

e. We ran for _____ when it started raining.

f. Building _____ are dangerous places.

g. I will neaten the _____ of the flowerbed.

h. The cheetah will chase its _____.

> I am sure I am **nocturnal**.

16. Use these words to make sentences of your own.

owls, **nocturnal**, **during**, **except**, **movements**, **quiet** and **trunks**.

17. Write the answers. Use the word list.

a. Write a word that has three syllables. _____

b. Write a word from the list that is in plural form. _____

c. Find smaller words in these words from the list:

during _____ **movements** _____ **sites** _____

d. Write a word that has **soft c**. _____

e. Which word starts and ends with a vowel? _____

f. Change one letter in each of these words to make words from the list:

owns _____ **pray** _____ **trucks** _____ **bites** _____

Talk about

18. Work with a friend. Recite the poem *Owl*.

Owl

Here is a bird of too few words,
Who never hoots for fun.
He finds the hoots of birds absurd,
And so he sticks to one.

The hoot and holler in the wood
Is din that hardly suits
The owl; and even though he could,
He doesn't give two hoots.

Christian Stevens

Key words are the most important words that are being written or said.

> **Example** The bold **child hid** behind the majestic oak **tree** in the hope that the teachers wouldn't find him.
> (The key words are in bold.)

19. Underline the key words in these sentences.

   a. The cheeky puppy has taken my favourite green slippers and has chewed them beyond recognition.

   b. I took the huge, leather-bound book off the shelf, blew off the dust and flicked through the flimsy, yellowed pages.

20. Read the text about owls again. In your copybook write the key words.

21. In your copybook write some facts about owls, using your key words to help you.

22. Below you will find a list of birds. Find smaller words in these words. Write them in your copybook.

> robin   starling   turkey   sparrow   finch
> pigeon   ostrich   parrot   dove   heron

Why is a lighthouse helpful?

1. Read the story.

Grace Darling

The weather was bad that day.
Storm winds blew and huge waves
crashed against the rocks.

William Darling was the keeper of
the Longstone lighthouse on the
coast of England. He looked out at
the storm and checked that all his
lights were working properly. These
lights would give warning to any
ships blown off course by the storm.
He saw a ship pass by and called to
his daughter, Grace. She looked out
the window at the ship and said,
'May God carry them safely through this storm.'

As night came, the storm grew worse. Grace and her parents could barely
sleep as the wind howled about the lighthouse. The sea roared below.

As the day broke, Grace looked out.

'Dad, come quickly!' she said. 'The ship we saw last night has broken into
pieces on the rocks.'

Grace and her father saw that there were nine people still alive on the rocks.
The Darlings decided that they would try and rescue them. The storm was
still raging when William and Grace set off in their little rowing boat. The
boat was tossed about in the rough waters. They struggled to row through
the waves. The survivors on the rocks could not believe their eyes. Who were
these brave people?

When William and Grace got closer to the survivors, William jumped onto
the rocks. Grace tried to keep the boat steady while five people climbed on
board. The boat could not hold any more people. The boat reached safety
and Mrs. Darling was there to help them. William and two of the survivors
went back to the rocks to save the other four. The survivors were very
grateful for the bravery of William and Grace Darling.

2. Talk about.

What do you think it means to be brave?

3. Answer the questions.

a.   Describe the weather at the lighthouse that night.

_____

b.   Where is the Longstone lighthouse?

_____

c.   Why did Grace call her father?

_____

d.   How many people could they see?

_____

e.   What kind of boat did they use?

_____

f.   What was the weather like during the rescue?

_____

g.   What happened to the people on the rocks?

_____

4. Complete the sentences.

a.   William _____ his lights were working properly.

b.   The lighthouse would give _____ to ships.

c.   The nine people _____ survive long on the rocks.

d.   The sea was very _____.

e.   Grace kept the boat _____ while the survivors climbed on.

f.   The _____ back to shore was dangerous.

g.   The survivors were _____ for the bravery of the Darlings.

5. In your copybook write the sentences in order.

A ship had broken into pieces. They rescued the survivors. William and Grace Darling set off in a rowing boat. There was a terrible storm. There were nine survivors on the rocks.

6. Answer these questions in your copybook.

a.   What would you have done if you had seen the survivors on the rocks?

b.   Would you like to live in a lighthouse? Give reasons for your answer.

69

A prefix is a group of letters at the beginning of a word which changes the meaning.

Sample re + write = rewrite

The prefix **un** means **not**.
The prefix **dis** means **opposite**.

Sample un + true = untrue
dis + order = disorder

7. Add **un** or **dis** to these words.

a.   do   _____
b.   agree   _____
c.   loyal   _____
d.   fit   _____
e.   obey   _____

f.   like   _____
g.   fair   _____
h.   lock   _____
i.   appear   _____
j.   tidy   _____

The prefix **pre** means **before**.
The prefix **re** means **again**.

Sample pre + war = prewar
re + build = rebuild

I am **un**happy about all this work.

8. Add **pre** or **re** to these words.

a.   cycle   _____
b.   heat   _____
c.   mature   _____
d.   historic   _____
e.   caution   _____

f.   view   _____
g.   visit   _____
h.   place   _____
i.   fill   _____
j.   play   _____

The prefix **mis** means **wrong** or **false**.
The prefix **non** means **not** or **opposite**.

Sample mis + use = misuse
non + smoking = non-smoking

9. Add **mis** or **non** to these words. Sometimes you will need a hyphen (-).

a.   -stick   _____
b.   behave   _____
c.   -stop   _____
d.   print   _____
e.   -fiction   _____

f.   sense   _____
g.   place   _____
h.   -flammable   _____
i.   trust   _____
j.   understand   _____

10. In your copybook write six sentences using words with prefixes.

Homophones are words that sound the same but have different meanings and spellings.

Sample I feel **weak** after my busy **week**.

Post the **mail**, not the **male**.

11. Circle the correct word then write the full sentence.

a. Kerry (would / wood) like to walk in the (would / wood).

_____

b. I (new / knew) I would get a (new / knew) bike.

_____

c. We've waited an (our / hour) for (hour / our) lunch.

_____

d. I hid my (whole / hole) wages in the (whole / hole) of a tree.

_____

e. He (threw / through) the ball (threw / through) the glass door.

_____

12. Write the homophones.

a. a set of two _____ a fruit _____
b. a dog can wag it _____ a story _____
c. opposite of female _____ post _____
d. ocean _____ your eyes do this _____
e. bucket _____ white _____
f. rob _____ a hard metal _____
g. it's like a rabbit _____ stuff on your head _____
h. not rich _____ do this with liquid _____
i. no war _____ a section _____
j. past tense of ride _____ street _____

Revision

13. Fill in pronouns to complete the sentences.

a. My cousins are coming to visit. I can't wait to see _____.
b. Our teacher thinks we are good. She will give _____ sweets.
c. Judy will ask _____ Mum if _____ can bake a cake.
d. My bed is warm and comfortable. I love sleeping in _____.
e. Do not touch that sandwich. It is _____.

There is more than one possibility for these. Compare your answers.

Word list

weather	lighthouse	against	coast	daughter	worse	below
survive	rough	storm	England	warning	roared	steady	rescue

14. Learn the spellings. Now look and say, picture, cover, write, check.

_____   _____

_____   _____

_____   _____

_____   _____

_____   _____

_____   _____

_____

15. Write any words you got wrong.

_____

16. Write the missing words. Use the word list.

a.   The pain in my foot got _____ when you stood on it.

b.   Do not speak on the telephone during a _____.

c.   A _____ warns ships of danger.

d.   The yacht sailed along the _____.

e.   The lion _____ when he saw me.

f.   It is tough to _____ in the desert.

g.   Elizabeth II is the Queen of _____.

h.   Sandpaper feels very _____.

Nice **weather!**

17. In your copybook use these words to make sentences of your own:
    weather, **against**, **daughter**, **steady**, **below**, **warning** and **rescue**.

18. Write the answers. Use the word list.

a.   How many words from the list have 1 syllable? _____

b.   How many words from the list have 2 syllables? _____

c.   Write the proper noun. _____

d.   Find smaller words in these words from the list:
    weather _____ **England** _____ **below** _____

e.   How many words from the list begin with **r**? _____

f.   Write two words with an **oa** pattern. _____ _____

g.   Underline the letter pattern that is the same in these words:
    lighthouse   daughter   rough

Talk about

19. Work with a friend. Tell each other the story from either William or Grace's point of view.

Write about

20. In your copybook write a story about a real-life hero that you have heard about. It can be a garda, a lifeguard, a fireman or an ordinary person.

> Tips for writing a story.
> ● Before you start your story, plan it.
> ● Where does it take place?
> ● Who are the characters?
> ● What happened?
> ● Make sure your story has a beginning, a middle and an end.
> ● Always read through your work to check it and improve on it.

> Grace Darling was born in 1815 and died of TB in 1842.

21. Complete the wordsearch.

D	a	r	l	i	n	g	s	l	x	w	c
a	s	d	w	w	f	s	h	i	p	a	g
y	t	G	e	a	r	u	e	g	w	r	q
q	b	r	a	v	e	r	y	h	j	n	m
w	e	a	t	e	e	v	s	t	h	i	n
r	b	c	h	s	r	i	a	h	g	n	b
t	h	e	e	t	t	v	r	o	u	g	h
s	z	a	r	o	y	o	q	u	f	l	v
q	f	j	o	r	u	r	e	s	c	u	e
h	g	f	p	m	i	s	w	e	d	k	c

weather	waves	Grace	warning
lighthouse	ship	survivors	rough
Darlings	storm	bravery	rescue

Before you read...

Are you good at making excuses? I hope not!

1. Read the poem.

The wolf's excuse

Would it be too crass
To apologise
To the girl, and her family, and you?
Yet – I was hungry,
And I'm a wolf,
It's what we do.

Gran was like leather,
Tough as old boots,
She had to be chewed with great care.
Then came the knocking
On the cottage door,
'Gran, are you there?'

You could call it greed.
I had eaten once,
And I shouldn't have taken the bait.
But here she was,
Fresh, tender young meat
On a red plate.

I believe it was fate
That brought her there,
And I ate her without much ado.
For I *was* hungry,
And I *am* a wolf.
It's what we do.

Yvonne Coppard

The story of Little Red Riding Hood was told by French peasants in the 14th century.

2. Talk about.

When might we make excuses? Remember the truth is always best!

3. Answer the questions.

    a. Who is speaking in the poem?

_____

    b. Who did the wolf eat first?

_____

    c. What kind of dwelling did Gran live in?

_____

    d. Who was knocking on the door?

_____

    e. What excuse does the wolf use?

_____

    f. What is the title of the poem?

_____

    g. Who is the poet?

_____

4. Answer the questions in your copybook.

    a. Why is the wolf apologising?
    b. Did he enjoy eating Gran? Explain your answer.
    c. Why do you think the girl was looking for Gran?
    d. Why couldn't the wolf resist eating her?
    e. Did the wolf do the right thing? Explain your answer.
    f. Give the poem another title.

5. Find words in the story with the same meaning. Use a dictionary.

    a. shocking   _____
    b. to say sorry   _____
    c. luck, destiny   _____
    d. material made from animal skin   _____
    e. fuss   _____
    f. rapping   _____
    g. gluttony   _____
    h. bribe / temptation   _____

A suffix is a group of letters at the end of a word.

> **Sample** hope – hope**ful**

6. Add **ment** or **ship** to these words. Write the new words.

a.	move	_____	f.	member	_____
b.	state	_____	g.	manage	_____
c.	partner	_____	h.	owner	_____
d.	govern	_____	i.	friend	_____
e.	content	_____	j.	champion	_____

7. Write a sentence using one of the **ment** or **ship** words.

   _____

If a word ends in **y**, change the **y** to an **i** before adding **ness**.

> Make yourself use**ful**!

> **Sample** lonely – loneliness

8. Add **ness** to these words.

a.	kind	_____	g.	fair	_____
b.	greedy	_____	h.	sad	_____
c.	tidy	_____	i.	nasty	_____
d.	happy	_____	j.	lovely	_____
e.	silly	_____	k.	fit	_____
f.	cold	_____	l.	weary	_____

9. Write a sentence using one of the **ness** words.

   _____

10. Add **ful** or **ly** to these words.

a.	hurt	_____	g.	neat	_____
b.	friend	_____	h.	hope	_____
c.	care	_____	i.	total	_____
d.	peace	_____	j.	slow	_____
e.	use	_____	k.	mad	_____
f.	glad	_____	l.	spite	_____

11. Write a sentence using one of the **ful** or **ly** words.

   _____

12. You need four colours. Underline four nouns in red, four verbs in blue, four adjectives in orange and two adverbs in green.

Wendy has a messy room. She tidies it seldom and her Mum gets quite angry. There are old magazines lying all over the floor. There are huge cobwebs hanging scarily from the ceiling. There is a mouldy sandwich under the bed waiting patiently for someone to find it.

13. Fill in adjectives and adverbs to make these sentences more interesting. Underline the adjectives in blue and the adverbs in green.
   a. The _____ boy ran _____ .
   b. The _____ donkey walked _____ down the hill.
   c. My _____ friend _____ gave me tea.
   d. My _____ pen is leaking _____ .
   e. His _____ ice-cream is melting _____ .
   f. The _____ lady spoke _____ to me.
   g. The _____ clouds moved across the sky _____ .
   h. The _____ nurse touched my arm _____ .

14. Rewrite the sentences adding capital letters, full stops and commas.
   a. i invited mark mollie kurt and jeff to my party in august.

   _____

   b. kelly's dog is fluffy cute and playful.

   _____

   c. the teacher's desk is covered in books pens papers and chalk.

   _____

   d. jackie and jay went to south america last christmas.

   _____

   e. this year i want my valentine to be peter jimmy and tom.

   _____

   f. the house on cherry road now belongs to mr. and mrs. kennedy.

   _____

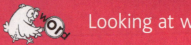
Word list

excuse	wolf	greed	hungry	leather	chewed	fate	care
cottage	eaten	shouldn't	bait	tender	believe	knocking	

15. Learn the spellings. Now look and say, picture, cover, write, check.

_____   _____
_____   _____
_____   _____
_____   _____
_____   _____
_____   _____
_____

16. Write any words you got wrong.

_____

17. Write the missing words. Use the word list.

   a.   You should take _____ when you cross the road.
   b.   Do you _____ there are ghosts in the school?
   c.   I went _____ on doors at Hallowe'en.
   d.   We have a _____ sofa in the lounge.
   e.   Have you _____ your lunch yet?
   f.   You _____ be talking during class.
   g.   I forgot to eat breakfast and I am _____.
   h.   The dog _____ the remote control.

> Mmm, I haven't **eaten** since this morning...

18. In your copybook use these words to make sentences of your own:
   excuse, **wolf**, **greed**, **fate**, **cottage**, **bait** and **tender**.

19. Write the answers. Use the word list.

   a.   Write the word **shouldn't** in full. _____
   b.   How many words have two syllables? _____
   c.   Find smaller words in these words from the list:
        leather _____ **cottage** _____ **tender** _____ **believe** _____
   d.   Write a noun. _____
   e.   Write the root words of these words:
        knocking _____ **chewed** _____ **eaten** _____

Talk about

20. Work with a group. Each person gives an excuse as to why his or her homework has not been done. Be creative (although usually you should not make excuses)!

Write about

21. In your copybook write an excuse poem explaining why you are so late for school. Write a new excuse on each line. Write about ten excuses and give your poem a title. Your poem does not have to rhyme.

> **Sample**
> *Why I am late for school*
> My budgie's cage needed cleaning,
> The tyre of the car was flat,
> There was a hole in my underwear,
> My poodle was attacked by a bat.

> Little Red Riding Hood in French is
> Le Petit Chaperon Rouge which means 'the little red hood.'

22. Work out the names of the fairytales.

   a. The Prog Frince   _____
   b. Back and the Jeanstalk   _____
   c. The Gree Gilly Boats Thruff _____
   d. Rindecella   _____
   e. The wisherman and his fife _____
   f. Beeping Sleauty   _____
   g. Boldilocks and the three gears _____
   h. Whow Snite   _____

A spoonerism is when the initial letters or sounds are swapped around.

> **Sample** big fox – fig box

23. Write two spoonerisms of your own.
   Little Red Riding Hood   _____
   The three little pigs   _____

Are you good when someone else is looking after you?

1. **Read the instructions.**

Babysitting instructions for: Michael

Outside playtime: 5.00pm – 5.30pm. He is not allowed to dig up the garden to make mud pies. Also make sure he does not climb the big tree as he cannot get down. The fire department is fed up with rescuing him.

Dinner: 5.30pm – chicken and vegetables in the microwave. (Do not let him have sweets or crisps for dinner.) He may have jelly if he eats all his dinner. (Make sure he doesn't feed his dinner to the cat.)

Television: He may watch TV from 6.00pm – 7.00pm. Please do not allow him to watch wrestling matches. They put him in a fighting mood and he will try to throw you to the ground.

Homework: 7.00pm – 7.30pm. He must do his reading, spellings and Maths. His work should be neat! He will ask you for all the answers – do not give them to him.

Bathtime: 7.30pm – 8.00pm. Please run a lukewarm bath for him. Remove all water guns from the bathroom. Pyjamas must be worn, not the Spiderman suit. He should not run around the house naked. School uniform should be hung up. He is not to go outside after his bath.

Bedtime: 8.00pm. Please read him a story. (No stories with wolves as these give him nightmares.)

General: Please give him lots of cuddles and kisses. He can be a good child, but please do not let him out of your sight.

Good luck! Thank you!

If you need us, we are at the Hillview Hotel, mobile number: 084-2578713.

2. **Talk about.**

    If you were babysitting young children, what extra care would you need to take?

3. **Answer the questions.**

    a. What is the name of the child?

    _____

    b. At what time should he do his homework?

    _____

    c. Why should he not climb the big tree?

    _____

    d. What puts him in a fighting mood?

    _____

    e. For how long may he watch TV?

    _____

    f. Which animals give him nightmares?

    _____

    g. What might he ask for during homework time?

    _____

    h. What type of dessert can he have?

    _____

    i. Where will the parents be?

    _____

4. **Answer the questions in your copybook.**

    a. What do you think the firemen think of this boy?

    b. Why do you think water guns should be removed from the bathroom?

    c. How long does homework and bath time take in total?

    d. Does he have a healthy dinner? Explain your answer.

    e. Do you think this child is good? Explain your answer.

    f. What would you do if a child that you were babysitting was bold?

5. **In your copybook write definitions for these words. Use a dictionary.**

    a. microwave   c. uniform

    b. jelly   d. nightmares

6. Write the missing prefixes.

un	mis	re	dis	non

a. Jeremy _____ likes fig jam.

b. You will need to _____ write this story.

c. I made a few _____ takes in my test.

d. Your spotty shirt is _____ usual.

e. It is good to read _____ -fiction books too.

f. You should not _____ behave in class.

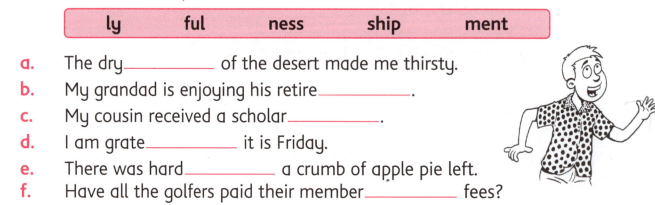

I thought these pans were **non-stick**!

7. Write one of the sentences.

_____

8. Add suffixes to complete the words.

ly	ful	ness	ship	ment

a. The dry_____ of the desert made me thirsty.

b. My grandad is enjoying his retire_____.

c. My cousin received a scholar_____.

d. I am grate_____ it is Friday.

e. There was hard_____ a crumb of apple pie left.

f. Have all the golfers paid their member_____ fees?

9. Write one of the sentences.

_____

10. Write the missing letter pattern.

ome	one

a. I have never been to R__ __ __.

b. The dog wants s __ __ __ b__ __ __s to bury.

c. Ph__ __ __ me when you get h__ __ __.

d. N__ __ __ of my friends will c__ __ __ to the disco.

e. Our garden gn__ __ __ has g__ __ __.

11. Write one of the sentences.

_____

An apostrophe and **-s** shows that something belongs to somebody.

> **Sample** The tractor belonging to Conor – Conor's tractor

Aoife's jumper is too big.

12. Add apostrophes. Rewrite the sentences in your copybook.
   a. We all wanted to ride Grahams bike.
   b. Jonathans party was a great success.
   c. They went to see Samanthas kittens.
   d. Neils runners are black and white.
   e. I am going to Anitas house for lunch.
   f. Seans trousers are ripped.
   g. The teacher read the pupils note.
   h. I would like to wear a policemans hat.

If a word already ends in an **s**, you still need to add an apostrophe and another **s**.

> **Sample** I want Lewis's hat.

13. Write a shorter version using an apostrophe.
   a. Boots belonging to James _____
   b. Scarf belonging to Janis _____
   c. Cat belonging to Rivus _____
   d. Work belonging to Des _____
   e. Chair belonging to Ross _____

If the word ends in **s** because it is a plural, then just put an apostrophe after the **s**.

> **Sample** the lions' den (more than one lion)

14. Add apostrophes. Rewrite the sentences in your copybook.
   a. Malcolms bedroom is covered in posters.
   b. The ladies hats were big and horrible.
   c. I want to borrow Jesss reading book.
   d. There are birds nests in the tree.
   e. The teachers staffroom is full of coffee mugs.
   f. The thieves bags were found outside.
   g. The girls plate is heaped with broccoli.
   h. The fairies wands could make you invisible.

The **teacher's** drawer is full of sweets.

Word list

chicken	babysitting	vegetables	watch	television
fighting	ground	remove	nightmares	hotel
mobile	allow	microwave	dinner	climb

15. Learn the spellings. Now look and say, picture, cover, write, check.

_____   _____

_____   _____

_____   _____

_____   _____

_____   _____

_____   _____

_____   _____

_____

16. Write any words you got wrong.

_____

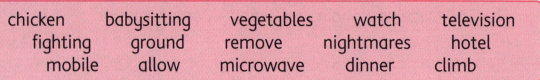

Kindly **remove** those boots!

17. Write the missing words. Use the word list.

a.   I hope you eat all your green _____.

b.   A _____ can warm up food quickly.

c.   I do not enjoy _____ my little sister.

d.   Do you _____ cartoons on TV?

e.   You should _____ your shoes before getting into bed.

f.   Mum will not _____ me to go out during the week.

g.   You may get_____ if you eat too much before going to bed.

h.   _____ those steep stairs carefully.

18. In your copybook use these words to make sentences of your own:
chicken, **television**, **fighting**, **ground**, **hotel**, **mobile** and **dinner**.

19. Write the answers. Use the word list.

a.   How many words have four syllables? _____

b.   Which word from the list has a **silent b**? _____

c.   Write two **ing** words from the list. _____

d.   Find smaller words in these words from the list:

   ground _____   **remove** _____   **hotel** _____   **allow** _____

Talk about

20. Work with a group. Each person should give instructions for doing something simple, such as making a drink, feeding the pets or brushing your teeth.

Write about

21. Write numbered instructions for the babysitter looking after you. Write your rough ideas here.

Instructions

_____

_____

_____

_____

_____

_____

_____

22. Read these jokes.

1. A young man volunteered to babysit one night so his mum could have an evening out. At bedtime he sent the youngsters upstairs to bed and settled down to watch football. One child kept creeping down the stairs but the young man kept sending him back. At 9pm, the doorbell rang, it was the next door neighbour, Mrs. Brown, asking whether her son was there. The young man brusquely replied, 'No'. Just then a little head appeared over the banister and a voice shouted, 'I'm here Mom but he won't let me go home.'

2. Babysitter (greeting the returning parents) 'Don't apologise for being late. If I had your two, I wouldn't be in any hurry to get back home either.'

23. Change one letter of each of these words so that they are words that appear in the jokes. There is more than one possibility for some.

went _____   batch _____   do _____   our _____

hen _____   ran _____   my _____   bring _____

rate _____   get _____   herd _____   ant _____

fang _____   four _____   neat _____

 Do you know of a place that has been named after a person?

1. **Read the story.**

How Rome got its name

Long, long ago, twins were born. One was named Romulus and the other was named Remus. Their mother loved them dearly.

But one night, an evil uncle, who did not want the twins around, took them away. He placed the twins in a basket and placed the basket in the River Tiber. He hoped they would be taken out to sea and lost forever.

The babies slept in the basket as it floated up the river. Some time later, the basket was stopped by a heavy branch in the water. The babies woke up and began to cry. They were cold and hungry.

A she-wolf heard the babies crying and went to investigate. She found the babies in the basket. Picking them up one by one, she took them back to her den. For many days she looked after them very well. She fed them, kept them warm and protected them from danger.

One night a shepherd passed near the wolf's den. He could hear the soft cries of the wolf cubs. But then he also heard the babies. He rushed to the den. The wolf did not move when he picked the babies up. She did not growl or try to stop him. The shepherd took the babies home. Romulus and Remus stayed with the shepherd until they were young men.

One day, Romulus said to his brother, 'I think we should build a city on the River Tiber.' Remus agreed.

As they were building the city walls, the brothers had an argument. Romulus became very angry. Then in a terrible rage, he threw a rock at Remus and killed him. With no-one to help him, it took Romulus a long time to build the walls. But at last the job was done.

'This city will be named after me,' said Romulus. 'It will be called Rome. It will one day be the greatest city in the world.' Rome did indeed become a powerful city that was one day to rule the world.

2. **Talk about.**

Discuss places that have possibly been named after people.

3. **Answer the questions.**

   a. What were the twins' names?

   _____

   b. What did an uncle do with the twins?

   _____

   c. What woke the babies?

   _____

   d. Who took the babies out of the basket?

   _____

   e. Who did the twins stay with until they were young men?

   _____

   f. Where did the brothers want to build a city?

   _____

   g. What happened to Remus?

   _____

4. **Complete the sentences.**

   a. The uncle hoped the twins would be _____ forever.

   b. The babies were crying in the basket because they were
       _____ and _____.

   c. The she-wolf _____ the babies from danger.

   d. The wolf did not _____ when
       the shepherd took the babies.

   e. In a terrible _____ Romulus
       threw a rock at Remus.

   f. Rome became a _____ city.

   g. The city of Rome is named after
       _____.

5. **Answer the questions in your copybook.**

   a. Why do you think the uncle did not want the twins around?

   b. What could have happened to the twins if the wolf had not
       rescued them?

   c. How do you think Romulus felt after killing Remus?

There are many words that have silent letters. In the word **know** the **k** is silent.

6. Write the missing **silent k** or **silent w**.

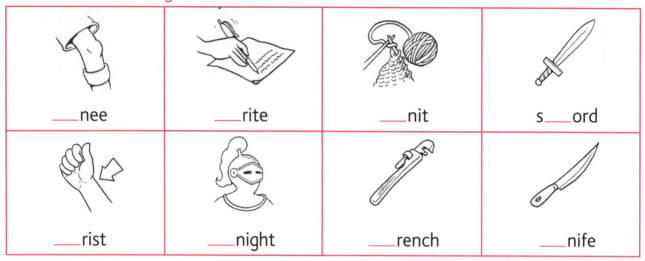

| ___nee | ___rite | ___nit | s___ord |
| ___rist | ___night | ___rench | ___nife |

7. Write the missing **silent b** or **silent l**.

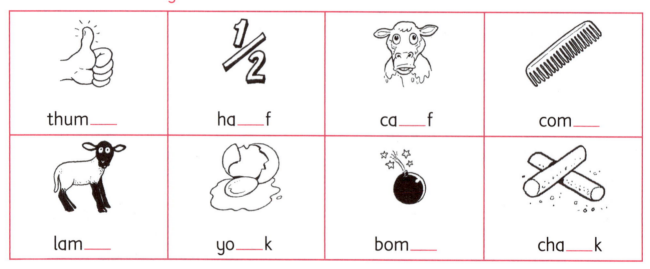

| thum___ | ha___f | ca___f | com___ |
| lam___ | yo___k | bom___ | cha___k |

8. Write the missing **silent g** or **silent t**.

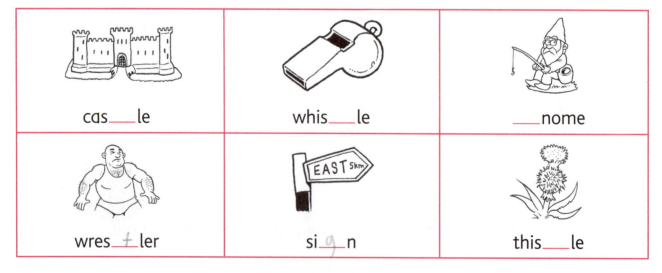

| cas___le | whis___le | ___nome |
| wres_t_ler | si_g_n | this___le |

9. Write six sentences in your copybook using words that have silent letters.

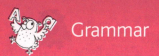
Speech marks show the words that people are saying.

| Sample | 'Hello,' Gary said. |

10. Write the conversation using speech marks.

Do you want to see my tarantula?

No thanks.

But I have it right here.

Get away from me!

'_____?' Gary asked.

Jill replied, '_____.'

Gary said, '_____,'

Jill screamed, '_____!'

> Speech marks go around the **actual words** people say.

If speech comes at the start of a sentence, put a comma at the end of it.

| Sample | 'I need some help,' said Ed. |

11. Add speech marks and commas.

a. Please explain said Mr. Brown.
b. I have lost my lunch money cried Robin.
c. The teacher has gone said Sheila.
d. You are late said Miss Reilly.
e. I know the answer said Meg.
f. Please write neatly said the teacher.
g. I will help you with your project whispered Billy.
h. Try to win this match pleaded the captain.

If speech comes at the end of a sentence, put a comma before the first speech mark and a full stop before the last one.

| Sample | Ed said, 'We need some help.' |

12. Add speech marks and commas.

> The speech part always starts with a capital letter.

a. Sophie said I hate shopping.
b. Patricia said I seem to be lost.
c. Lena said We must play football at break.
d. Sue said The teacher will be back any minute.
e. The teacher said Stop talking and work.

Word list

twins	evil	uncle	basket	babies	protected	growl
agreed	terrible	rage	powerful	floated	threw	taken	heavy

13. Learn the spellings. Now look and say, picture, cover, write, check.

_____   _____
_____   _____
_____   _____
_____   _____
_____   _____
_____   _____
_____

14. Write any words you got wrong.

_____

15. Fill in the missing words. Use the word list.

   a.   We _____ the litter in the dustbin.
   b.   My _____ is my mother's brother.
   c.   Two babies born together are called _____.
   d.   My schoolbag is too _____ to carry.
   e.   Have you _____ your friends out to tea?
   f.   The balloon _____ away with the breeze.
   g.   The panda bear is a _____ species.
   h.   The _____ were crying and keeping me awake.

16. In your copybook use these words to make sentences of your own:
    evil, basket, growl, agreed, terrible, rage and **powerful.**

Who **threw** that?

17. Write the answers. Use the word list.

   a.   Find smaller words in these words from the list:
        basket _____ **growl** _____ **agreed** _____ **rage** _____

   b.   Count the number of syllables in each word:
        babies _____ **protected** _____ **terrible** _____ **powerful** _____

   c.   Write a word from the list that has double letters:

        _____

Talk about

18. Work with a group. Act out the story *How Rome got its name*. You will need people to play Romulus, Remus, their mother, the uncle, the she-wolf and the shepherd.

Write about

19. Create an imaginary town named after you or part of your name. In your copybook write ten sentences about the town.

> Tips for writing about your imaginary town:
> ● Where is your town?
> ● Hot big is it?
> ● What facilities does it have?
> ● Does it have public transport?
> ● Does it have any natural features, e.g. rivers?
> ● What makes your town special?
> ● Mention the name of the town.

20. Tell each other about your towns.

> The Roman name for Ireland was Hibernia.

21. Match the places to the people they were named after.

Tasmania	George Washington
San Francisco	King Phillip of Spain
Pittsburgh	King George I
Louisiana	James Monroe
Saudi Arabia	William Pitt the Elder
The Bronx	Abel Tasman
Washington	Queen Victoria
Georgia, USA	King Louis XIV of France
Pennsylvania	St. Francis
Queensland	Mohammed Bin Saud
Monrovia	James Bronck
Philippines	William Penn

22. Name three places in Ireland that have been named after a person.

Before you read... You will need your own food label for this lesson.

Do you read the labels on your food products? You should!

1. Look at the labels on these food products.

BARNEY'S Beans IN BARBECUE SAUCE ✓

Cooking instructions: Hob: bring gently to the boil, stirring. Microwave: heat in the microwave for two minutes and stir.

420g

yum yum CHOC SPREAD

300g

Ingredients: sugar, vegetable oils, cocoa powder, milk powder, flavouring

Perfect Pasta

Made from 100% durum wheat

BEST BEFORE 06/2009

Nutritional information: (per 100g)
Energy 1434kj, Protein 12g
Carbohydrates 68g, Fibre 5g
Fat 2g, Iron 1.6mg

500g ✓ V Suitable for vegetarians

♻ = recycle	V = suitable for vegetarians
	mg = milligrams
	g = grams
✓ = low salt	kj = kilojoules

2. Talk about.

Talk about the food labels you have brought in.
Why should we read them?

3. Answer the questions.

a. What kind of sauce does *Barney's Beans* have?

_____

b. How long should you microwave the beans for?

_____

c. How much does the chocolate spread weigh?

_____

d. Does the chocolate spread contain milk products? Explain your answer.

_____

e. How much protein would be found in 200g of pasta?

_____

f. What is the pasta made from?

_____

g. What do these stand for?

g _____   mg _____   kj _____

4. Look at your own food label and write the answers in your copybook.

a. What is your product called?
b. How much does it weigh?
c. Name two ingredients in the product.
d. Write out the bar code.
e. Name the food company that makes this product.
f. Are there any serving or cooking instructions?
g. Write some other information given on the label.

5. What do these stand for?

a.   _____   d. _____

5 00 1 2 54 67 7 880 1 4 3

b. Best before   _____

c. V   _____   e. _____

The letters **wa** can have different sounds.

> **Sample** **was** or **walk**

6. Write the missing letters.

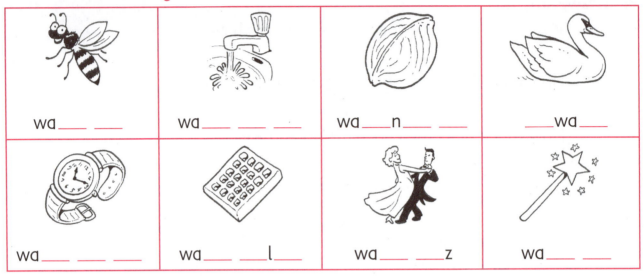

| wa___ ___ | wa___ ___ ___ | wa___n___ ___ | ___wa___ |

| wa___ ___ ___ | wa___ ___l___ | wa___ ___z | wa___ ___ |

7. The letters **wa** can make different sounds. Sort the words by their sound.

> wasp   water   walnut   swan   watch   waffle   waltz   wand

wa as in was	**wa** as in water

8. Write the missing **wa** letters. Underline them in red if they sound like **was**. Underline them in blue if sound like **water**.

  a.   Do not ___ ___nder off.
  b.   That light bulb is 60 ___ ___tts.
  c.   Do not go over the ___ ___terfall.
  d.   I ___ ___nt to ___ ___lk the dog.
  e.   ___ ___sh the ___ ___sp carefully.

9. Write six sentences in your copybook using **wa** words. They can be silly! Example: The **wa**lnut **wa**ltzed with the **wa**ffle.

When we write verbs in the past tense sometimes we add **ed**.

> **Sample** play – **played**

If the word has a short vowel sound we double the last letter.

> **Sample** stop – sto**pp**ed

> **Remember:** It is the verb that changes with the tenses.

If a word ends in **e** we just add **d**.

> **Sample** like – lik**ed**

Sometimes verbs have their own special past tense.

> **Sample** write – **wrote**

10. Write the past tense of these verbs.

a. fly - _____   i. buy - _____
b. dig - _____   j. sleep - _____
c. speak - _____   k. go - _____
d. run - _____   l. throw - _____
e. ride - _____   m. make - _____
f. see - _____   n. know - _____
g. rip - _____   o. receive - _____
h. meet - _____   p. take - _____

11. Underline the verbs in these sentences. In your copybook rewrite these sentences in the past tense.

a. The policemen come and catch the thieves.
b. I go to horse riding and bring my riding hat with me.
c. My Mum digs in the garden and makes a vegetable patch.
d. People say that I am very good looking.
e. The teacher thinks that the pupils are noisy.
f. The artist draws and sketches on canvas.
g. The birds eat seeds and drink water.
h. The children choose a topic and write about it.

12. Underline the verbs in this paragraph. Rewrite it into the past tense in your copybook.

Triceratops is a horned dinosaur. It has three sharp horns and a bony frill. The horns are its best defence and cause damage to its predators. It grows up to nine metres long and weighs over five tons. It lives in North America and it grazes in large herds. It is a powerful dinosaur.

Word list

| sauce | cooking | gently | stirring | spread | sugar | powder |
| wheat | protein | iron | fibre | energy | information | boil | oils |

13. Learn the spellings. Now look and say, picture, cover, write, check.

_____   _____
_____   _____
_____   _____
_____   _____
_____   _____
_____   _____
_____

14. Write any words you got wrong.

_____

15. Fill in the missing words. Use the word list.

a.   Mum is _____ lasagne for dinner.

b.   _____ some butter on your scone.

c.   You should rock the baby _____.

d.   I like mint _____ with my lamb.

e.   Bread is made from _____.

f.   _____ is used to sweeten foods.

g.   Get your _____ for the project from the library.

h.   I will _____ some cabbage for your dinner.

> I think that's too much **sugar!**

16. In your copybook use these words to make sentences of your own:
    stirring, powder, protein, iron, fibre, energy and **oils**.

17. Write the answers. Use the word list.

a.   Find smaller words in these words from the list:

    spread _____ **wheat** _____ **iron** _____ **information** _____

b.   Count the number of syllables in each word:

    protein ____ **information** ____ **energy** ____ **powder** ____

c.   Write the root words for these words from the list:

    cooking _____ **stirring** _____ **gently** _____

d.   Write a word from the list that has a **silent r.** _____

Talk about

18. Work with a friend. Tell each other about the product label you have brought in.

Write about

19. In your copybook design a label for a chocolate spread.
Remember to include all the information and give it a name.

> Tips for designing a label.
> - Include the name of your product.
> - Give a list of the ingredients.
> - Make sure the packaging is eye-catching.
> - Give the weight of the product.
> - Include the company name.
> - Include the expiry date.
> - Include the bar code.
> - Include the nutritional information.

> Look out for preservatives and colouring in your food.
> Too much of these are not good for you.

20. Spot the ten differences.

Dinosaur 100g

FRUIT GUMS

Fruit flavour chewy gums

Ingredients: glucose syrup, sugar, fruit and vegetable extract, citric acid, flavourings

Produced in Germany for Dinosaur Dinners Ltd. Phone us: 18904321543

5 00 1 2 54 67 7 880 1 43

Per sweet:
Energy: 75kj, Protein: 0.4g
Carbohydrate:4.0g

Best before Sept 2008

Dinosaur 100kg

FRUIT GEMS

Fruit flavour chewy gums

Ingredients: glucose, sugar, fruit and vegetable extract, citric acid, flavourings

Produced in Germany for Dinosaur Diners Ltd. Phone us: 18904312543

5 00 1 2 54 67 7 880 1 44

Per sweep:
Energy: 75kj, Protein: 0.04g
Carbohydrate:4.0g

Bets before Sept 2008

 Do you enjoy eating out?

1. **Read the poem.**

Sky in the pie

Waiter, there's a sky in my pie
Remove it at once if you please
You can keep your incredible sunsets
I ordered mincemeat and cheese

I can't stand nightingales singing
Or clouds all burnished with gold
The whispering wind is disturbing the peas
And making my chips go cold

I don't care if the chef is an artist
Whose canvases hang in the Tate
I want two veg. and puff pastry
Not the Universe heaped on my plate

OK I'll try just a spoonful
I suppose I've got nothing to lose
Mm... the colours quite tickle the palette
With a blend of delicate hues

The sun has a custardy flavour
And the clouds are as light as air
And the wind a chewier texture
(With a hint of cinnamon there?)

This sky is simply delicious
Why haven't I tried it before?
I can chew my way through to Eternity
And still have room left for more

Having acquired a taste for the Cosmos
I'll polish this sunset off soon
I can't wait to tuck into the night sky
Waiter! Please bring me the Moon!

Roger McGough

The pie has been around since the Ancient Egyptians from 2000 BC.

2. Talk about.

Have you ever been disappointed by a meal?
What is the best way to complain?

3. Answer the questions.

a. What did the person order?

_____

b. Why does he complain at first?

_____

c. What is making his food go cold?

_____

d. Which birds are mentioned in the poem?

_____

e. What other interest does the chef have?

_____

f. What does the sun taste like?

_____

g. Which ingredient has a hint of cinnamon?

_____

h. Who wrote the poem?

_____

4. Answer the questions in your copybook.

a. What is the 'Tate'? *art gallery*
b. What is puff pastry used for? *covers the pie*
c. Why do you think the person decided to try the food?
d. Name the ingredients he tasted.
e. How did his mood change in the poem?
f. How do you imagine the clouds, moon and sun would taste?

5. Find words in the story with the same meaning. Use a dictionary.

a. take away _____

b. someone who cooks _____

c. mixture _____

d. taste _____

e. the way something feels _____

f. obtained, got _____

6. Sort the words by their **ch** sound.

chorus   chauffeur   match   monarch   reach
chevron   champion   orchestra   chateau

ch as in chop	**ch** as in chemist	**ch** as in chef

7. Write the correct letter patterns.

amp   ump

> Use your dictionary.

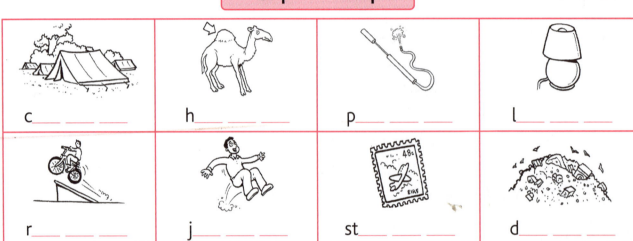

c _ _ _ _ _   h _ _ _ _ _ _   p _ _ _ _ _   l _ _ _ _ _

r _ _ _ _ _   j _ _ _ _   st _ _ _ _ _   d _ _ _ _ _

8. Write six sentences in your copybook using **amp** and **ump** words.

9. Write the missing word endings.

er   or   ar

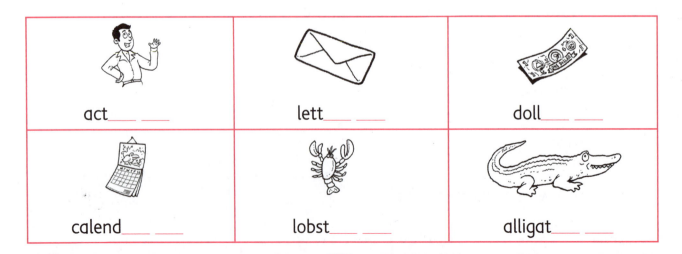

act _ _ _ _   lett _ _ _ _   doll _ _ _ _

calend _ _ _ _   lobst _ _ _ _   alligat _ _ _ _

Remember: contractions are words that are shortened. The apostrophe is used where letters are left out.

> **Sample** was not – wasn't

10. Add apostrophes. Rewrite the sentences.

a. Bobs work is always neat.

_____

b. Im going to school in Alans bus.

_____

c. The fairies wands werent working.

_____

d. Theyre taking Johns bike.

_____

e. Its raining and Harrys skateboard is getting wet.

_____

f. Mandys Mum cant collect her from school today.

_____

g. The puppies tails arent wagging.

_____

h. The ladies coats werent warm enough.

_____

11. Add speech marks. Write the new sentences in your copybooks.

a. I don't like living in this cage said the bird.
b. Jack said I'd love to go in a space rocket.
c. The chef asked Has anyone seen my tomatoes?
d. I will make you a banana sandwich said Danny.
e. Michael screamed Do not touch that wet paint!
f. The teacher announced Play time is over.
g. Look both ways before you cross the road warned Dad.
h. Can I go home early? asked the tired child.

12. Rewrite this paragraph in the past tense.

We go for a drive on Sundays. Dad drives and Mum reads the map. Shauna sings her head off. Matt eats and drinks non-stop. It is a horrible journey.

_____

_____

_____

_____

Word list

simply	sunsets	ordered	chef	artist	universe	spoonful
suppose	blend	flavour	hint	delicious	taste	polish	waiter

13. Learn the spellings. Now look and say, picture, cover, write, check.

_____   _____
_____   _____
_____   _____
_____   _____
_____   _____
_____   _____
_____   _____
_____

14. Write any words you got wrong.

_____

15. Fill in the missing words. Use the word list.

   a. Just a _____ of sugar helps the medicine go down.

   b. This apple pie tastes _____.

   c. The _____ gave me the menu.

   d. The _____ made a hearty Irish stew.

   e. An _____ often paints on canvas.

   f. You should _____ that wooden table.

   g. I _____ I could buy you a meal.

   h. We _____ steak and chips.

16. In your copybook use these words to make sentences of your own:
   simply, **sunsets**, **universe**, **blend**, **flavour**, **hint** and **taste**.

17. Write the answers. Use the word list.

   a. Write two words from the list that have an **ou** pattern.

       _____   _____

   b. Do they sound the same? _____

   c. Write two words from the list that have a **sh** sound.

       _____   _____

   e. Write a verb (action word) from the list. _____

   f. Change one letter in each of these words to make words from the list:
       pint _____   **tasty** _____   **waited** _____

Did you **polish** your shoes?

Talk about

18. Work with a group. Recite the poem *Sky in the pie* in your groups. Use expression. Write out your own part. Practise a few times before presenting it to the class.

Write about

19. Write a poem about finding something strange in your pie. Ideas for 'ingredients' could be a shop, farm, zoo, town or school. Give your poem a title. It does not have to rhyme. Do your rough work here.

_____

_____

_____

_____

_____

_____

_____

_____

_____

_____

_____

20. Check your poem carefully. Write it out neatly, add a picture of your pie and display it.

> A shoofly pie is a pie filled with molasses, which is a sweet, sticky substance.

21. These pies are all mixed up! Unscramble the letters to find out what's inside.

a. keats and nidkey pie _____

b. eseech pie _____

c. kincech and mooshrum pie _____

d. cinme pie _____

e. efeb and nooni pie _____

f. palep pie _____

g. dum pie _____

h. heshperds pie _____

i. krop pie _____

j. tatoop pie _____

Before you read...

Have you heard of the Salmon of Knowledge?

1. **Read the story.**

Fionn and the Fianna

The Fianna lived in Ireland many, many years ago. They were brave warriors. If you wanted to join the Fianna, you had to pass certain tests.

- Run through a forest without breaking a single stick under your feet.
- Jump over a branch as high as yourself.
- Run under a stick set at the height of your knee.
- Know twelve books of poetry off by heart.
- Pick a thorn from your foot while you run at top speed.
- Promise to obey the rules of the Fianna.

When Fionn was a boy he was sent to an old poet called Finnegas to learn poetry. One day the old poet caught a very special fish. This fish was the Salmon of Knowledge. Whoever tasted the fish first would get the gift of wisdom.

Finnegas told Fionn to cook the fish, but he warned him, 'Do not taste the fish! I must be the first person to taste it!' Fionn cooked the fish over a fire. While he was cooking it, he burned his thumb on the fish. He put his thumb into his mouth to ease the pain. He had tasted the Salmon of Knowledge!

Finnegas came back and Fionn told him what had happened. 'You are very wise now,' said the old poet. 'You must go to Tara and become leader of the Fianna.'

Fionn went to Tara. It was the feast of Samhain. The high king and the Fianna were having a banquet. However, they were not happy, but fearful. At this time each year a fiery monster burnt the palace down. As the monster came near the palace he would play sweet music which made all the warriors fall asleep.

Fionn said, 'I am going to stop this monster. If I do, you must make me leader of the Fianna.' The high king agreed.

Fionn took his magic spear and waited. Soon he heard beautiful, sweet music and his eyes started to close. He felt very sleepy. 'I must stay awake!' he said. He pressed the spear into his forehead and the pain kept him awake.

Fionn attacked the monster and killed him. 'You are the greatest warrior in Ireland,' said the high king to Fionn. 'You shall be leader of the Fianna.'

2. Talk about.

What do you think it means to be wise?

3. Answer the questions in your copybook.

   a. Who were the Fianna?
   b. Name one test you had to pass to join the Fianna.
   c. Why was Fionn sent to Finnegas?
   d. What was special about the fish Finnegas caught?
   e. How did Fionn get to taste the fish?
   f. Where did Fionn have to go?
   g. Why were the Fianna and the king fearful?
   h. What did Fionn do?

4. Complete the sentences.

   a. Finnegas caught a fish called the _____.
   b. Finnegas wanted to be the _____ person to taste the fish.
   c. Fionn was told that he should become _____ of the Fianna.
   d. When Fionn went to Tara, it was the feast of _____.
   e. The monster would play _____ to make the warriors fall asleep.
   f. Fionn stayed _____ by pressing his spear into his forehead.
   g. Fionn _____ the monster and became leader of the _____.

 Use a dictionary.

5. Find words in the story with the same meaning.

   a. fearless _____
   b. soldier _____
   c. a large formal meal _____
   d. a place where royalty lives _____
   e. someone in charge of a group of people _____
   f. advise, caution someone _____

6. Answer the questions in your copybook.

   a. How do you think Finnegas felt when Fionn tasted the fish?
   b. What do you think it means to be wise?

7. Fill in the missing silent letters. Write the full sentence in your copybook.

w	k	g	b	l

   a. Stay ca____m during a fire drill.
   b. My feet have gone num____ from the cold.
   c. Did you ____rap my present yet?
   d. Your pet rat will ____naw those wires.
   e. Turn the door ____nob and go in.

8. Add a suffix. Write the full sentence.

ful	ly	ness

   a. The sweet_____ of this toffee makes my teeth sore.

   _____

   b. Please be care_____ when swimming.

   _____

   c. I real_____ like your stripy trousers.

   _____

   d. Lee was very thank_____ for the scooter.

   _____

   e. You must do this work proper_____.

   _____

9. Add a prefix. Write the full sentence.

re	dis	un

   a. The monster is so far _____seen.

   _____

   b. We will need to _____build the wall after the storm.

   _____

   c. Mum said she would _____connect the Internet.

   _____

   d. Teachers are never _____kind.

   _____

   e. You will need to _____mix those paint colours.

   _____

10. You have been given a list of things to do. In your copybook write a diary entry in the past tense explaining what you had to do.

- Take the money and the list.
- Go to Dunnes Stores and buy a lettuce, tomatoes and salad cream.
- Go to the post office and get ten stamps.
- Check to see if Gran needs anything.
- You can have €2 to get yourself something.
- Go to the bus stop and catch the number 12 bus to get to Aunt Milly's.
- I will meet you there.

11. Add apostrophes. Rewrite these sentences in your copybook.

a. Camillas toys are lying everywhere.

b. The babies mothers are talking about nappies.

c. Were going to watch a video at Laras house.

d. I didnt take my brothers sleeping bag.

e. The classs projects havent been completed.

f. Dad shouldnt borrow the neighbours tractor.

g. Hes cleaned the hamsters cage.

h. Jamess sister wouldnt tidy her room.

12. Add speech marks, commas, full stops, capital letters, question marks and exclamation marks. Rewrite the sentences in your copybook.

a. i would like prawns for lunch said billy

b. where do you think you are going asked the teacher

c. pam said its too windy to go outside

d. vegetables are good for you explained Mum

e. can i go to dublin on saturday asked bob

f. your dinner is ready now called Mum

g. neil cried she has ruined my picture

h. i haven't taken your pencil lied shelley

Word list

warrior	certain	breaking	poetry	obey	whoever
thumb	knowledge	wise	fearful	burnt	music
	leader	awake	happened		

13. Learn the spellings. Now look and say, picture, cover, write, check.

_____   _____

_____   _____

_____   _____

_____   _____

_____   _____

_____   _____

_____

14. Write any words you got wrong.

_____

15. Fill in the missing words. Use the word list.

 a. There are _____ chores that should be done every day.

 b. He was a strong and brave _____ in the war.

 c. If you read _____ your reading will improve.

 d. I enjoy listening to classical _____.

 e. Children must _____ the school rules.

 f. I made dinner but I _____ the rice.

 g. What _____ to your shirt?

 h. The owl looks like a _____ bird.

> I am **fearful** of the dark.

16. In your copybook use these words to make sentences of your own:

 breaking, **whoever**, **thumb**, **knowledge**, **fearful**, **leader** and **awake**.

17. Write the answers. Use the word list.

 a. Find smaller words in these words from the list:

 warrior _____ **leader** _____ **music** _____

 b. Write the root words of these words from the list:

 breaking _____ **fearful** _____ **leader** _____

 c. Which word from the list has a **silent b**? _____

 d. Break the word **whoever** into two words. _____ _____

Talk about

18.   Work with a group. Act out the story of *Fionn and the Fianna*.

Write about

19.   In your copybook write a series of tests that you would need to complete to become leader of the classroom.

20.   Follow the instructions to complete the picture.
    1.   Below the large cloud, in the middle, draw three birds flying.
    2.   Colour the hills in green.
    3.   Draw four purple flowers along the river bank, near Fionn's right foot.
    4.   Draw the sun in the middle of the sky and colour it yellow.
    5.   Just under the salmon, draw another small fish jumping out of the water.
    6.   Colour the grass in the foreground two different shades of green.
    7.   Add your own touches to the picture!

Gill & Macmillan

http://www.gillmacmillan.ie

Copyright © Janna Tiearney 2007
Commissioning Editor: Helen Dowling
Managing Editor: Maggie Greaney
Publishing Consultant: Gay Judge
Designer: Derry Dillon
Print Origination: Design Image
Illustrator: Derry Dillon

First published April 2007.

978-1-84450-092-5

Acknowledgements:
Two witches discuss good grooming by John Coldwell used by permission of Macmillan Children's Books, London, UK.
Owls, a poem by Christian Stevens (Wolfhound Press, 2001) reproduced by permission of Wolfhound Press, an imprint of Merlin Publishing, Dublin. © Christian Stevens 2001.

Every effort has been made to trace copyright holders but we would be glad to rectify any omissions at the next reprint.

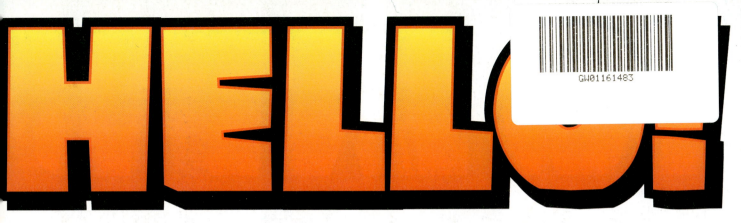

HELLO!

CALLING ALL BLOX HEADS!

WELCOME TO YOUR ULTIMATE GUIDE TO ALL THINGS *ROBLOX*!
PACKED FULL OF TOP TIPS, GAMER GUIDES, YOUTUBER INTERVIEWS,
LOLS AND MORE. GET READY TO JOIN US ON AN
EPIC *ROBLOX* ADVENTURE!

ROBLOX ROCKS!

DC THOMSON

EXPORT DISTRIBUTION (excluding AU and NZ) Seymour Distribution Ltd, 2 East Poultry Avenue, London EC1A 9PT Tel: +44(0)20 7429 4000 Fax: +44(0)20 7429 4001 Website: www.seymour.co.uk

Enquiries: editor@110%gaming.com

WHAT'S

EXPLORE

- **6** WORLD OF ROBLOX
- **20** A-Z OF ROBLOX
- **30** GREAT GAME GENERATOR
- **98** DID YOU KNOW?

GREAT GAMES

- **32** GET SPOOKED
- **37** IF YOU LIKE...
- **60** ROBLOX REPLAY
- **66** WHICH TYCOON?

P82 A DAY WITH DENIS

BLOX ON!

INSIDE!

★ ★ ★ ★ ★ ★ ★ ★ ★ ★ ★ ★ ★ ★ ★ ★ ★ ★ ★ ★

TIPS & TRICKS

18 JAILBREAK VS. FLEE THE FACILITY

22 MAKE A GAME

27 DOS & DON'TS

LOL ZONE

10 JUST KIDDING

25 BRILL BREWS

46 BLOXY BINGO

84 BLOX HEADS

P49 100 THINGS TO DO IN ROBLOX

TYCOONS RULE!

THE W🌍RLD OF
ROBLOX
EVERYTHING A ROBLOXIAN NEEDS TO KNOW!

LET'S EXPLORE!

With millions of different games and experiences for you and your mates to try out, there's definitely something for everyone on Roblox!

NICE TO MEEP YOU!

AWESOME OBBY!

Obstacle courses – or obbies – are so much fun! Whether you're escaping a crazy maze or speed-running through lots of levels, you're bound to up your gaming reflexes as you become a platformer pro!

IF YOU'RE *OBBY* AND YOU KNOW IT!

BUILD A CITY!

Make the world of your dreams, **Roblox** style! Whether you want to get a job, go to school, run a farm, build a mega mansion, or even just hang out with your friends, there's a city sim for you - awesome!

COIN YOU BELIEVE IT?

SO SPOOKY!

If jumpscares are your thing, **Roblox** has you covered! With games like **Doors**, **Spider** and **Piggy**, you'll be able to put your nerves to the test and show that you're the bravest **'Bloxer** around!

TOP TYCOONS!

The aim of the game is simple – make money! There are so many tycoons to try, starting out small then growing your business into a massive empire! Have you got what it takes to reach the big time?

MEGA MANSION TYCOON

BEST OF THE REST!

There's just so much to do in Roblox! From playing your fave sports, riding on rollercoasters, and adopting the cutest pets, to bossing the best minigames, driving slick sports cars, and embarking on epic adventures – you'll never run out of fun things to try!

WHICH GAME SHOULD YOU PLAY?

Answer these questions to find out!

ADD UP YOUR SCORE!

YOUR FAVOURITE GAMES ARE...

1 Fantasy-filled
2 Packed with minigames
3 Open world
4 Full of action
5 Competitive

AT A SLEEPOVER, YOU'RE...

1 Already fast asleep
2 Snacking and chatting
3 Watching movies
4 Playing games
5 Pulling pranks

PICK A SNACK...

1 Strawberry milkshake
2 Chocolate cake
3 Pizza
4 Nachos
5 Spicy wings

YOU'D LIKE TO BE KNOWN AS...

1 Being kind to others
2 Giving the best advice
3 Cracking funny jokes
4 Having lots of energy
5 Being brave

ADOPT ME! `4-9`

From raising adorable pets to decorating an awesome house, we think you'll LOVE Adopt Me! There's loads of variety and the cuteness factor is off the charts!

MEEPCITY `10-15`

MeepCity is a great game pick for every social butterfly! You can hang out with your friends and play minigames and, best of all, adopt customisable Meeps!

JAILBREAK `16-20`

So, you're all about the action, eh? Jailbreak is the game for you! Whether you're committing a heist or stopping the criminals, we promise you won't be bored!

CITY LIVING!

BUILD YOUR OWN DREAM ROBLOX WORLD WITH THESE GREAT GAMES!

MEEPCITY

Hang out with your mates and build your dream estate in MeepCity! With loads of minigames to play, an awesome avatar editor and the most adorable Meeps to adopt, there's always something fun to get up to in this epic experience.

LIVETOPIA

From choosing your own outfits, to picking the purrfect pet, you can truly make the world of Livetopia your own. Why not live a life of luxury in a fancy apartment, or maybe try out the simple life at a farm in the countryside?

BERRY AVENUE

Whether you decide to enrol in the local high school or start working in the grocery store, there's absolutely loads to get stuck into in Berry Avenue! Maybe you want to help the residents and become a doctor, or maybe you want to cause some chaos and rob a bank – it's up to you!

REDCLIFF CITY

Roleplay your way and make **Redcliff City** your own! You could drive and explore in a super-cool sports car, invite your friends to tour the home of your dreams, or even put on a fashion show with loads of amazing accessories.

EMERGENCY RESPONSE: LIBERTY COUNTY

If you want a world jam-packed full of action, look no further! There are so many different roles to play as, from a heroic firefighter to a criminal on the run so there's always a fun new way to play. With a huge world to explore, there's loads to discover – including a secret mountain hideout!

BLOX THE DIFFERENCE!

■ **Can you find all six differences between the two pictures below?**

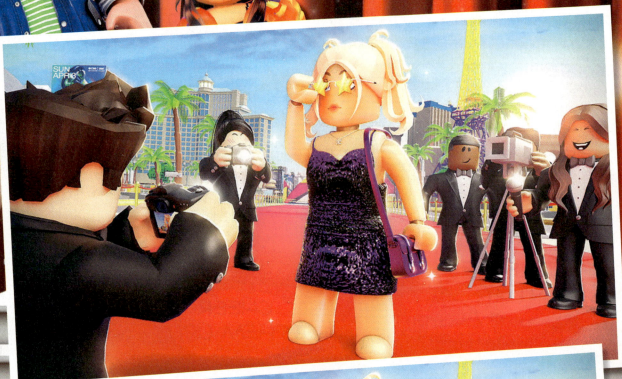

ANSWERS

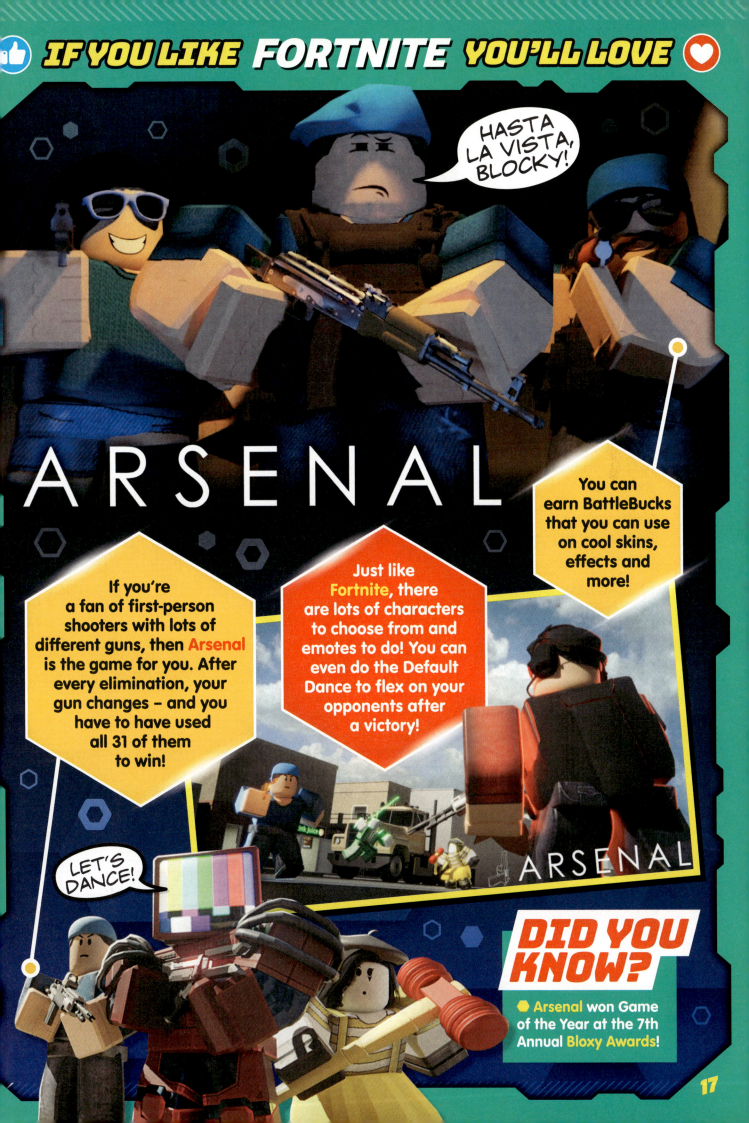

HASTA LA VISTA, BLOCKY!

ARSENAL

You can earn BattleBucks that you can use on cool skins, effects and more!

If you're a fan of first-person shooters with lots of different guns, then Arsenal is the game for you. After every elimination, your gun changes – and you have to have used all 31 of them to win!

Just like Fortnite, there are lots of characters to choose from and emotes to do! You can even do the Default Dance to flex on your opponents after a victory!

LET'S DANCE!

ARSENAL

DID YOU KNOW?

Arsenal won Game of the Year at the 7th Annual Bloxy Awards!

17

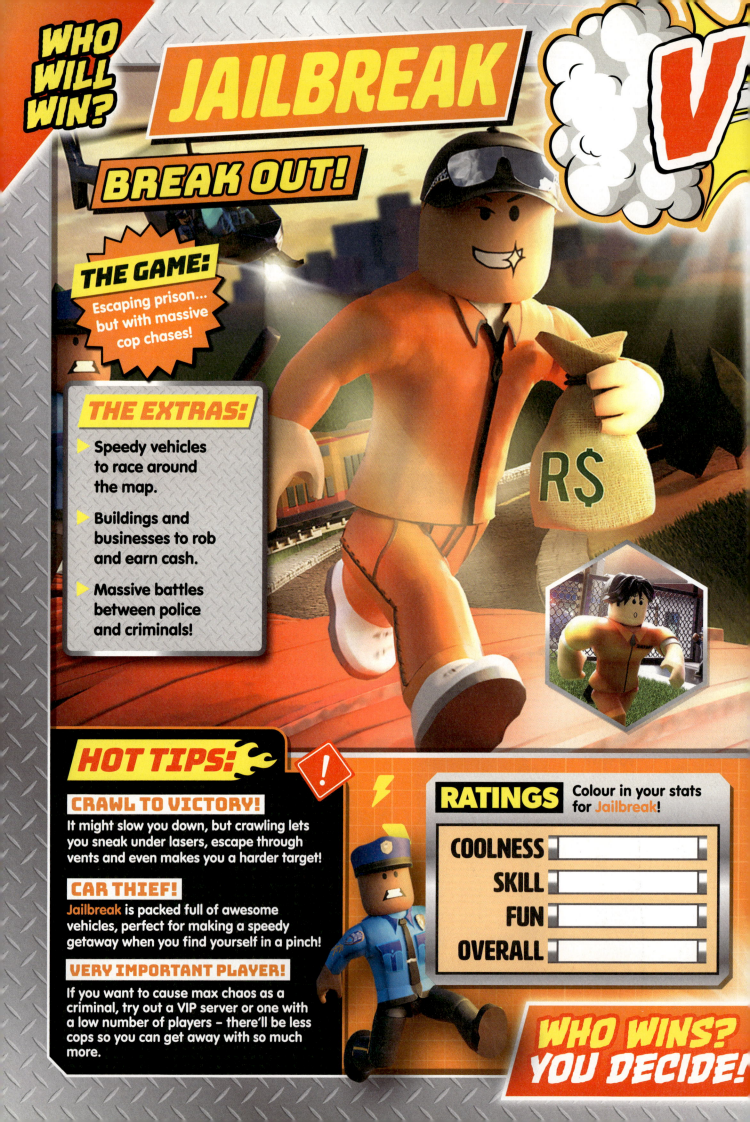

WHO WILL WIN?

JAILBREAK

BREAK OUT!

THE GAME:
Escaping prison... but with massive cop chases!

THE EXTRAS:
- Speedy vehicles to race around the map.
- Buildings and businesses to rob and earn cash.
- Massive battles between police and criminals!

R$

HOT TIPS:

CRAWL TO VICTORY!
It might slow you down, but crawling lets you sneak under lasers, escape through vents and even makes you a harder target!

CAR THIEF!
Jailbreak is packed full of awesome vehicles, perfect for making a speedy getaway when you find yourself in a pinch!

VERY IMPORTANT PLAYER!
If you want to cause max chaos as a criminal, try out a VIP server or one with a low number of players – there'll be less cops so you can get away with so much more.

RATINGS
Colour in your stats for Jailbreak!

COOLNESS	
SKILL	
FUN	
OVERALL	

WHO WINS? YOU DECIDE!

FLEE THE FACILITY

HOT HACKS!

THE GAME:

Hacking... But with an evil Beast!

THE EXTRAS:

▶ Customisable hammers and gems to battle in style.

▶ Skill checks to keep you on your feet.

▶ Loads of maps to explore and escape from!

HOT TIPS:

STICK TOGETHER!

Hacking all the computers on each map takes ages. If you team up with fellow players to hack the same device, you'll drastically increase the speed for completion!

GLOWING MARKER!

The loud scary music lets you know the Beast is nearby, but it doesn't tell you where they're going to appear. If you watch the walls and doors, you can spot a red glow surrounding the Beast, giving you the heads-up needed to hide!

JUMP AND SLIDE!

The Beast is faster than you, so you need to use your wits to escape! It can't go through small gaps, and jumping objects takes serious time, so when making your escape, always try to crawl through vents, jump over counters and go through windows!

RATINGS

Colour in your stats for Flee the Facility!

COOLNESS

SKILL

FUN

OVERALL

19

A-Z OF ROBLOX

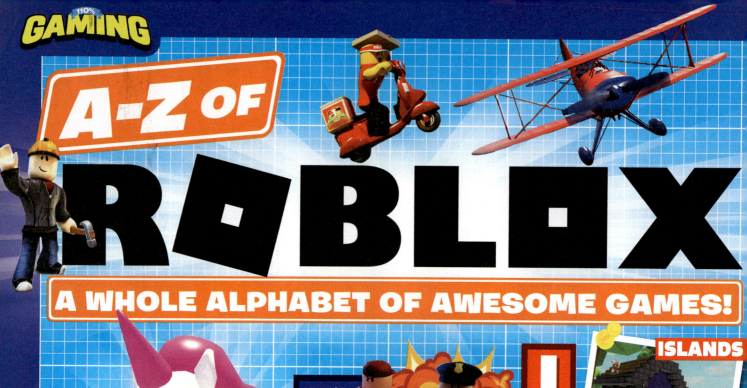

A WHOLE ALPHABET OF AWESOME GAMES!

A
ADOPT ME!
All the cute pets!

B
BROOKHAVEN
Explore this amazing city!

C
CAR CRUSHERS 2
Ultimate destruction!

D
DEMONFALL
Fight to survive!

E
EMERGENCY RESPONSE: LIBERTY COUNTY
Nee naw, coming through!

F
FLEE THE FACILITY
Run away!

G
GREENVILLE
So many cool cars!

H
HIDE & SEEK EXTREME
Come out, come out, wherever you are!

I
ISLANDS

J
JAILBREAK
Goodie or baddie, your call!

K
KING LEGACY

L
LOOMIAN LEGACY
One for Pokémon fans!

M MEEPCITY
The coolest place to hang!

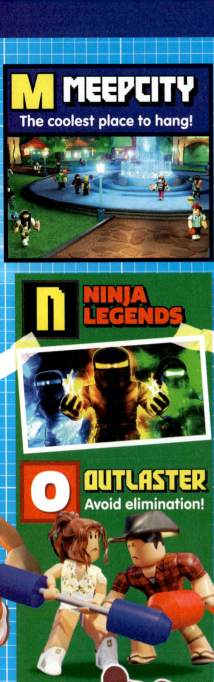

R ROYALE HIGH
School's never been so cool!

N NINJA LEGENDS

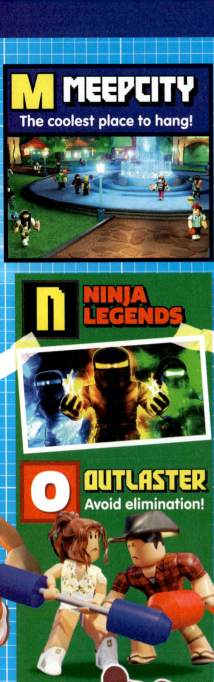

S STRUCID
Epic Battle Royale!

X XMAS UPDATES
All the best games get an Xmas update!

T TOWER DEFENSE SIMULATOR

O OUTLASTER
Avoid elimination!

U UK:RC REDWOOD COUNTY
Keep the world safe!

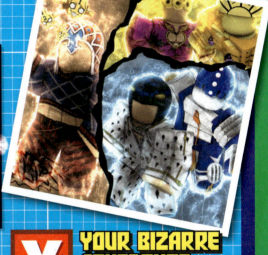

P PIGGY

V VR HANDS
High five! 👋

Y YOUR BIZARRE ADVENTURE
Ace RPG action!

Z ZOMBIE UPRISING

W WELCOME TO BLOXBURG
Build your own world!

Q Q-CLASH
Battle it out!

BRRRAAAIIINS!

ALL THE TIPS YOU NEED TO MAKE YOUR OWN *OBBY* IN *ROBLOX!*

MAKE A ROBLOX GAME!

GETTING STARTED!

"Install Roblox Studio, then go to Roblox.com/create and click on Start Creating. Click New in the panel on the left, then click on Baseplate to open up a new project file. Make sure you have the Explorer and Properties windows open. If you don't see them, click on the View tab in the menu at the top to select them."

Studio
Make Anything You Can Imagine
With our FREE and immersive creation engine

Start Creating
Manage my games

ROBLOX STUDIO IS FREE ON WINDOWS AND MAC!

SPAWN AREA!

STEP 1 "Build a Lobby area where players will spawn by clicking the Home tab, then the Part button. To make the part big enough, set the Size to 35,1,35 in the Properties tab."

STEP 2 "Click on the Model tab, and then click Spawn in Gameplay. This will insert a SpawnLocation. Use the Move and Scale tools to position your SpawnLocation on top of the Part so it's big enough for multiple players to spawn at once."

STEP 3 "Delete the Baseplate so players can't walk on it and cheat the obby! Select the Baseplate inside the Explorer panel and then right click and click Delete."

IMPORTANT! MAKE SURE ALL PARTS ARE ANCHORED, SO THEY DON'T FALL OUT THE MAP WHEN THE GAME LOADS! SELECT EACH PART IN THE EXPLORER PANEL AND TICK THE ANCHORED PROPERTY.

ALVINBLOX TAKEOVER

JUMP SET!

STEP 1 "To make your first obstacle select the part underneath the SpawnLocation, then right click and select Duplicate. Use the move tool to drag it away. This will create a clone of the part which we can now scale down into a jump. Select the Scale tool and drag the handles until it looks more like a rectangle."

STEP 2 "When you've created your first jump, you can keep Duplicating and moving them along until you have a set. To finish this obstacle, select the platform at the start, duplicate it and move it to the end of the jumps."

CHOOSE PATH!

STEP 1 "Insert a new part into the game, then click and drag it so it's against the platform we just created. Use the Scale tool to make it a long path which you can walk across. Repeat this two more times so you have three paths next to each other."

STEP 2 "Click on each path, then set its CanCollide property to either be checked or unchecked. If it's checked then the player will be able to walk over it. If it is unchecked, they will fall through it! You should have two unchecked paths and one checked path."

SELECT A PART AND CHANGE THE BRICKCOLOR OR COLOR PROPERTY TO CHANGE ITS COLOUR!

DON'T LOSE YOUR HEAD!

23

BALL JUMPS!

STEP 1

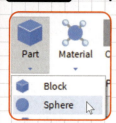

"Add another platform to separate this obstacle by duplicating the one from the previous step. Then click on the arrow underneath the Part button and click Sphere. This will insert a ball into our game. Scale it and drag it to where you want the jump to be."

STEP 2

"Duplicate the ball, then use the Move tool to position it away from the first one. Repeat as many times as you like. Make sure that the gap isn't too big and that it's still possible to jump from one ball to the other. Move the balls to the left or right to add more challenge."

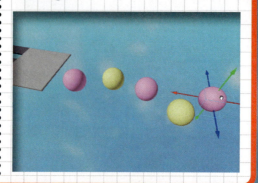

FINISHING TOUCHES!

STEP 1

"Add one more part and scale it so that it's big enough to fit multiple players on. This is going to be the winners' section, where you can hang out once you've completed the obby!"

STEP 2

"You can decorate your winners' section by adding models from the Toolbox. Click the Toolbox button in the Home tab of the Menu and search for a model. Once you've found one you'd like to insert, just click it and it will insert itself into your game. Use the Move and Scale tools to position it in place."

STEP 3

"To publish your game to Roblox, click the File button in the top left corner and then click Publish to Roblox As. Give it a name and add a description if you wish, then click Create. Once published, click Close, then click Game Settings in the Home tab of the menu. Under the Permissions tab, set the Playability to Public or Friends. If you only want your Roblox friends to be able to play the game you can set it to Friends only, or Public if you want anyone to be able to play it. Then click the Save button."

NOW YOU CAN FIND YOUR GAME ON ROBLOX AND PLAY IT!

MEET THE MAKER!

NAME: AlvinBlox
WHO: YouTuber and Roblox Creator
SUBS: 477K

ACHIEVEMENTS:
● Member of the Roblox Video Star Program.
● Officially recognised Roblox Featured Educator.
● Bloxy Award Winner for Community Contribution.

HAVE A GOOD KNIGHT!

*Figures correct at time of print

BRILLIANT BREWS!

There are nearly 150 potions to choose from in **Roblox Wacky Wizards**, so we've made it easier to pick your next brew! Simply spin a pencil to reveal what your next potion should be!

YOUR WACKY WIZARDS RECIPE GUIDE!

CREEPER
Become a Creeper and the rest will be HISStory!
YOU WILL NEED:
Eggcano
Dynamite

GHOSTLY
Boo! Don't scare yourself when you turn into a ghost!
YOU WILL NEED:
Bird
Spider

BUZZING
Because who doesn't want bee wings!
YOU WILL NEED:
Bird
Honey

FIREWORK
Become a firework and make Katy Perry proud!
YOU WILL NEED:
Pool Noodle
Dynamite

KABOOM
Your attacks are DYNAMITE!
YOU WILL NEED:
Dynamite
Boxing Gloves

SPIDER-MAN
Sling webs and save the city!
YOU WILL NEED:
You
Spider

SLINKY
Become a human... well, Roblox slinky!
YOU WILL NEED:
Pool Noodle
Disco Ball

DISCO BODY
You ARE the party!
YOU WILL NEED:
Disco Ball
Brain
You

RATTY
Make all your rodent dreams come true!
YOU WILL NEED:
Spider
Witches Brew

EXPLODING SQUIRTS
This is exactly as it sounds... we wish we had goggles!
YOU WILL NEED:
Rotten Sandwich
Dynamite

TIP!
ADD A POOL NOODLE TO THIS RECIPE AND SEE WHAT HAPPENS!

JUNGLE ADVENTURE

WHAT GAME WILL YOU MASTER?

START

CHOOSE YOUR FAVE JUNGLE ANIMAL:

GORILLA → **WHAT'S MORE IMPORTANT IN A GAME?**

TIGER → **PICK A FRUIT:**

ACTION → **WHAT SOUNDS MORE FUN?**

THE STORY → **YOU'RE ALWAYS...**

MANGO

PINEAPPLE

JUNGLE SAFARI

KAYAKING → **YOU'RE ALWAYS...**

YOU'D RATHER SLEEP IN A...

TREEHOUSE

ON TIME → **WHICH ROBLOX GAMES DO YOU PREFER?**

IN A HURRY → **GAMES WITH MULTIPLE ENDINGS ARE...**

TENT

WHAT BEST DESCRIBES YOU?

TYCOONS

ESCAPE OBBIES

ADVENTUROUS

INTERESTING

NOT FOR ME

CREATIVE

THE JUNGLE STORY

You're super-daring and are always up for a challenge. Making it through this interactive story game isn't easy, but we think you have what it takes!

THE JUNGLE OBBY

You're very adventurous and like games that keep you on your toes. You can do anything you put your mind to - like escaping this **Roblox** jungle!

JUNGLE TYCOON

You've got the patience and creativity needed to design your own tropical jungle. It'll be hard work but will be worth it in the end!

⚠ THE DOS & DON'TS OF... ⚠

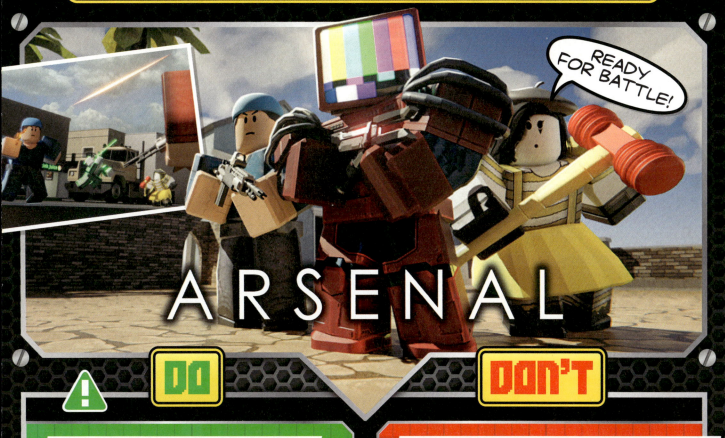

READY FOR BATTLE!

ARSENAL

DO

DON'T

MELEE MANOEUVRES!

⚠ Getting to the battlefield is key to bagging a swift victory, however heavy weapons can really slow you down. If you're not in combat, make sure to have your melee equipped so you can dash at super-speed!

GROUP UP!

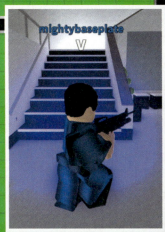

mightybaseplate

⚠ Heading into fights one after the other will just result in your team making no progress. Instead, try to coordinate a big push or just follow another player – double the firepower means double the chance of winning!

BOUNCE AROUND! ⚠

⚠ Some weapons, including the golden melee, have an epic ability that lets you double jump! This means that even if you don't have a good weapon, you can leap into the air to dodge fire and gain a height advantage, helping you to take that W!

RUN DOWN HALLWAYS!

⚠ The best way to keep yourself out of danger is to run around in the open, jumping all over the place and moving in unpredictable ways. This can't be done in a narrow hallway or alley, so entering a fight in these spots without some quick thinking will only result in an even quicker failure! ⚠

STEAL FROM FRIENDS!

⚠ As fun as getting the final blow on an enemy might be, if your teammate did all the work in the first place, let them finish the job. Stealing that victory just isn't cool! ⚠

GET MAD!

⚠ At the end of the day, it's just a game with super-quick rounds and quick action. Sure, it can get annoying if you start to stack up the Ls, but it's no big deal – there's always next round!

27

WHO WILL WIN?

ADOPT ME!

ADOPT 'EM ALL!

THE GAME:
Families... but with little pets to collect!

THE EXTRAS:
- ▶ Chores to help your pets grow.
- ▶ Customisable houses to live in.
- ▶ Fun events to keep things fresh.

LET'S BE PENG PALS!

ADOPT ME!

HOT TIPS:

KIDS RULE!
To earn extra money, switching to a child lets you complete additional chores to take care of yourself!

GROWTH SPURTS!
Common pets grow up way faster, so if you're looking to get an adult quickly, stick with the easy ones!

RAPID NEONS!
If there is an event with pets available, collect loads of the cheapest and easiest pets – you can use them to make super-rare neons really quickly!

RATINGS
Colour in your stats for Adopt Me!

COOLNESS	
SKILL	
FUN	
OVERALL	

WHO WINS? YOU DECIDE!

PET SIMULATOR X

PERFECT PETS!

PAWSOME!

THE GAME:
Animals... but they're miners?!

THE EXTRAS:
- Lots of unique lands to travel to.
- Tradeable pets and items.
- Rewards to unlock through progress.

RATINGS
Colour in your stats for **Pet Simulator X**.

COOLNESS	
SKILL	
FUN	
OVERALL	

HOT TIPS:

KEEP ON HATCHIN'!
The more eggs you hatch, the better your mastery will become, and a high mastery can get you discounts on super-expensive eggs!

MORE THE MERRIER!
Collecting coins can be easy peezy if you have a buddy. Not only does it give you a coin boost, but it also can be more fun!

LUCK IS ON YOUR SIDE!
When trying to get rarer pets, make sure to have luck boosts enabled so you can increase your odds of getting a super-rare and awesome new pet!

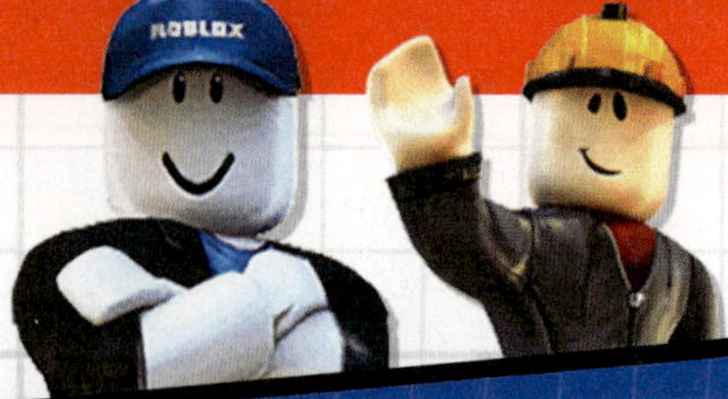

GREAT GAME GENERATOR!

Find out which **Roblox** game you should play next!

START

You love simulation games!

YES → You can spend hours on a game!

YES →

NO

NO

You're a big puzzle fan!

NO

Roblox is your fave game ever!

NO

YES

NO

It's every player for themselves!

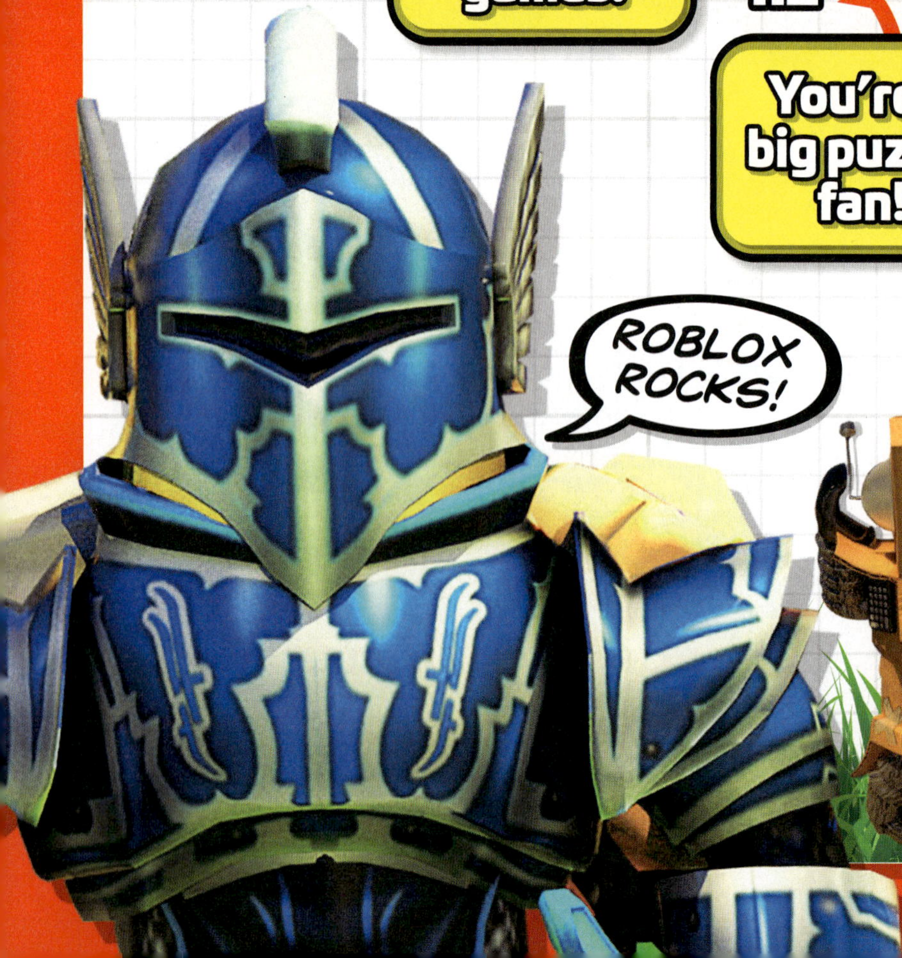

ROBLOX ROCKS!

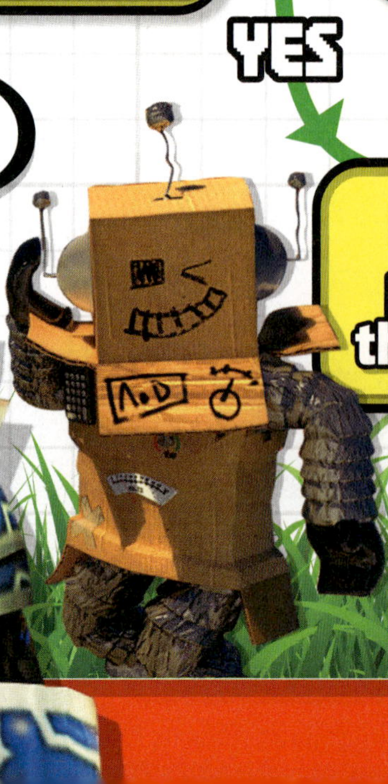

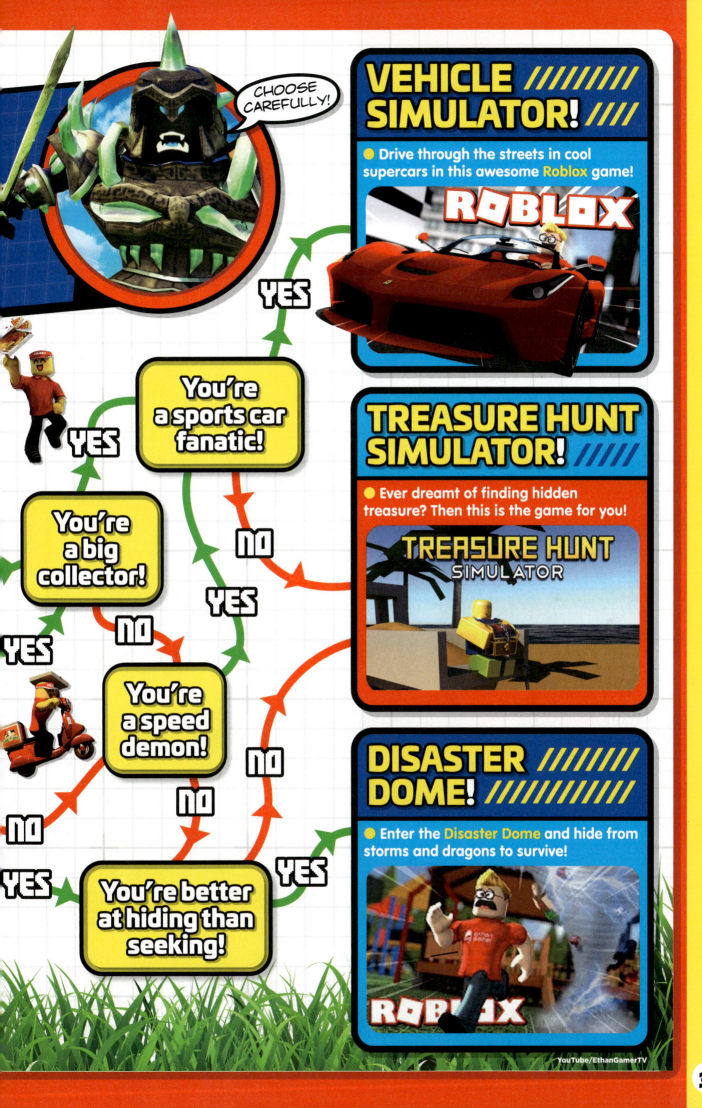

CHOOSE CAREFULLY!

YES

You're a sports car fanatic!

YES

NO

YES

You're a big collector!

YES

NO

You're a speed demon!

NO

NO

NO

YES

YES

You're better at hiding than seeking!

VEHICLE SIMULATOR! ///////// ////

● Drive through the streets in cool supercars in this awesome **Roblox** game!

ROBLOX

TREASURE HUNT SIMULATOR! /////

● Ever dreamt of finding hidden treasure? Then this is the game for you!

TREASURE HUNT SIMULATOR

DISASTER DOME! ///////// ///////////

● Enter the **Disaster Dome** and hide from storms and dragons to survive!

ROBLOX

YouTube/EthanGamerTV

31

GET SPOOKED!

PREPARE FOR A SCARE WITH THESE CREEPY GAMES!

SPIDER

Solve puzzles, collect keys and avoid the Spider as you try to escape each map without being bitten! Each round, a different player will take a turn at playing as the Spider but with loads of different skins to choose from, you can totally make this creepy crawly your own!

PIGGY

Play your way through each chapter of this spooky story, uncovering the game's mysteries as you go. With a whole host of different game modes to choose, from Infection to Tag, as well as two books to play through, Piggy will keep you on the edge of your seat for ages!

RAINBOW FRIENDS

This might look like a cute and colourful game, but don't be fooled! When your trip to a theme park goes wrong, you must collect items to get through each night and escape the creepy Rainbow Friends!

RIVERRIDE THROUGH
HEMLOCK WOODS

DOORS

Explore the hotel and work your way through rooms one to 100 on your mission to escape! Each room you enter is randomly generated, so you'll never have the same experience twice as you work your way through. Watch out for who might be lurking behind each door!

APEIROPHOBIA

You never know what to expect from Apeirophobia's creepy levels! Will they be safe? Will they be scary? Solve the puzzles and find out for yourself! The more you play and get to know the different entities, the longer you'll last next time you log on.

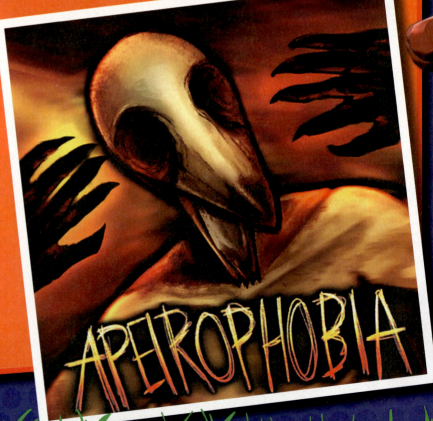

FLEE THE FACILITY

Can you avoid the Beast and escape the map without being frozen?! Hack computers, unlock doors, hide and sneak your way out of the facility. Or, you can take a turn playing as the Beast, using your special hammer to freeze foes!

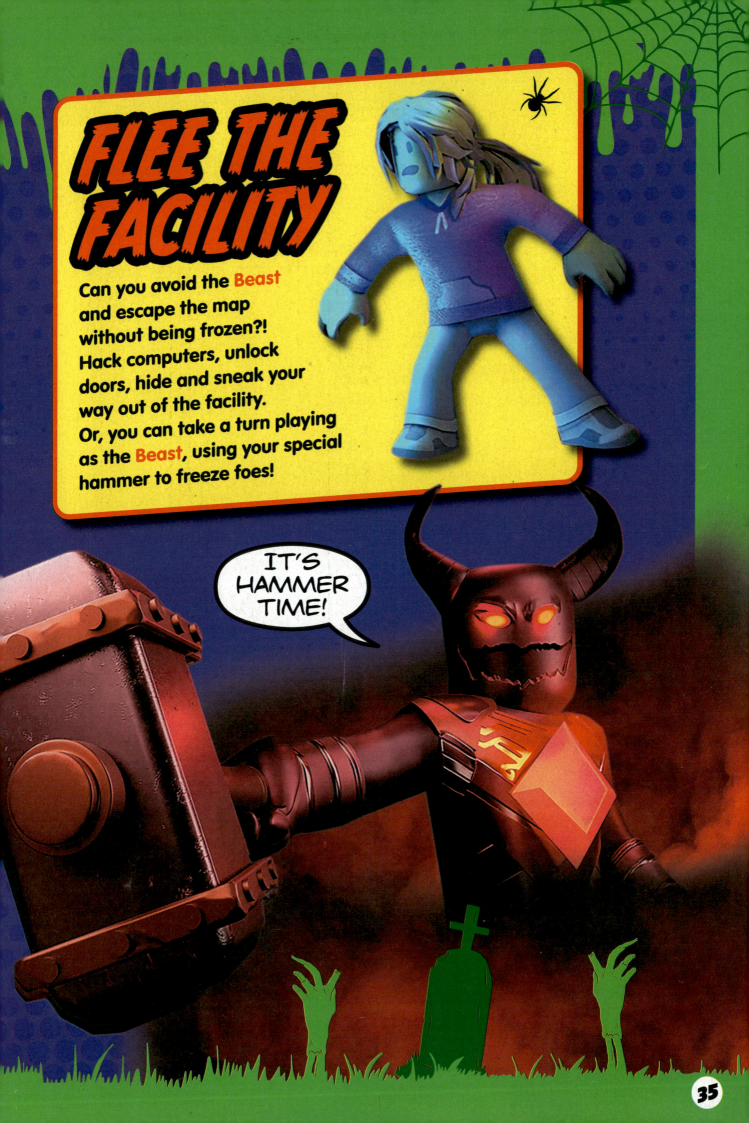

COSMAZE!

COSMINUS IS ESCAPING THE LAB! QUICK, HELP OVERDRIVE CATCH UP TO HIM!

IT'S NOT OVER!

START

FINISH

YOU CAN'T CATCH ME!

WHAT DO SUPERHEROES PUT IN THEIR DRINKS?

JUST ICE!

ANSWER:

36

DOORS

💻 📱 ⊗

DOORS is a spooky horror game that can only be found on **Roblox**!

KNOCK, KNOCK!

There's a Guiding Light trying to help you solve puzzles, locate keys and stay on the right path, so make sure you pay attention to what it's trying to tell you!

Can you and your friends get out of the haunted hotel? Watch out for creatures like **Timothy** and **Glitch** and you just might make it out!

SCARY WARNING!

⬡ **DOORS** is only for the bravest of the brave gamers, so be prepared for a scare before you play!

ROYALE HIGH

COOL SCHOOL!

THE GAME:
School... but you're magical!

ROYALS RULE!

THE EXTRAS:
- ▶ Classes to attend and learn.
- ▶ A house to live in and have fun.
- ▶ Outfits to make you look like royalty!

HOT TIPS:

HOW LOW CAN YOU GO?!
A fun way to earn diamonds is by going to the disco and doing the cool limbo minigame! You will gain some sweet rewards if you can complete it!

SET A REMINDER!
You can unlock cool prizes like diamonds and items by logging in every day. To help you remember this, you could set a reminder on your phone or a sticky note on the fridge!

NIGHTY NIGHT!
When your energy is low, make sure you head to the bed in your house asap, as when you gain the energy, you also gain XP! This also allows you to have a little short break from the intense life of a prince or princess!

RATINGS
Colour in your stats for Royale High.

COOLNESS
SKILL
FUN
OVERALL

WHO WINS? YOU DECIDE!

BROOKHAVEN

BRILL BUILDS!

BROOKHAVEN

THE GAME:

A neighbourhood... where you can do anything!

THE EXTRAS:

- ▶ Toys and accessories to play with.
- ▶ Tough trophies to earn.
- ▶ Fantastic furniture to unlock and decorate.

BROOK BFFS!

RATINGS

Colour in your stats for **Brookhaven**.

COOLNESS	
SKILL	
FUN	
OVERALL	

HOT TIPS:

EXPLORE!

Looking for something to do? The world is filled with secrets and cool areas for you to find! Take a look around and solve puzzles; maybe you will be surprised at what you have found!

LOCK THE DOORS!

If people keep breaking into your house and messing around with your stuff, don't panic! Make sure you lock the doors when you are out and about or when you're inside so that only people you want to enter can!

TIME FOR A MAKEOVER!

If you're playing the role of a doctor, wearing a silly outfit just won't cut it! You can customise your character for free by pressing the avatar editor button in the game!

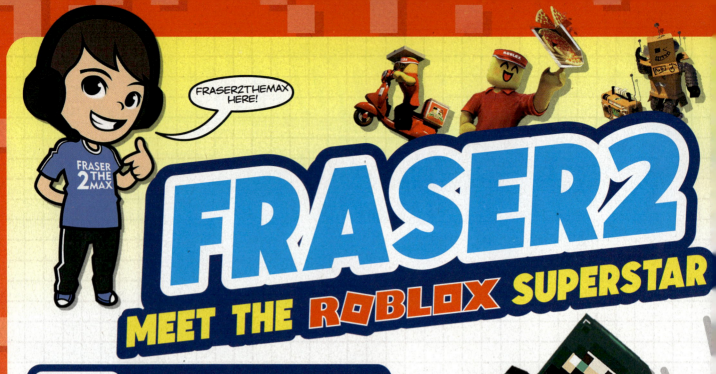

FRASER2THEMAX HERE!

FRASER2
MEET THE ROBLOX SUPERSTAR

NAME: Fraser2TheMax
SUBS: 69.3K
PLAYS: Lots of Roblox!

HOW DID YOU GET INTO ROBLOX?

"I was looking for cool games to play and I came across it. MeepCity is my favourite!"

HOW DID IT FEEL TO BE THE ROBLOX STREAMER OF THE WEEK?

"Amazing, I was really happy to be picked considering my age."

DID YOU KNOW?

Fraser presented an award at the Roblox Bloxy Awards!

WHAT'S THE MOST RANDOM THING THAT EVER HAPPENED TO YOU IN ROBLOX?

"I was filming a video and ThnxCya turned up and was also filming a vid but I thought it was a fake ThnxCya... until I watched the vid on his channel and there I was!"

THE MAX

Quick Fire Round!

FRASER'S NO.1 ROBLOX TIP!

MEEPCITY RACING

"Stay near the edges in MeepCity Racing and if you ever come across a point where you have the choice of a lucky block or a speed boost, go for the speed boost!"

WHAT HAS MADE YOU LOL MOST WHILST GAMING?

"When doing a collab with SallyGreenGamer she got stuck in a secret room I showed her because the item she was wearing was too big to get out the door!"

CHECK OUT FRASER'S CHANNEL AT F2TM.COM

SHREK OR MINIONS?
"Shrek!"

TV OR YOUTUBE?
"YouTube."

BATMAN OR SUPERMAN?
"Batman!"

MINECRAFT OR ROBLOX?
"Roblox!"

DONUT OR ICE CREAM?
"Donut!"

IRON MAN OR SPIDER-MAN?
"Iron Man!"

BATHE IN BAKED BEANS OR SWIM IN MUD?
"Bathe in baked beans!"

FRASER2THEMAX

ROBLOX ROUND UP!

GAME: FORGET YOUR FRIEND'S BIRTHDAY

WHAT IS IT?

"In this game you wake up to realise you haven't got your friend a birthday cake! Or any presents for that matter! Luckily, you're a great friend (even though you forgot), so you must quickly scramble to get the best cake and coolest gift for their birthday. On your quest you can solve puzzles, find secrets, and explore the world!"

You
OH NO! I TOTALLY FORGOT ABOUT THAT!

BEST BIT!

"My favourite part of this game is all the different things you can control and play with – you can call someone on the phone to come and explode your door in case you get locked inside your house, or you could give some chips to your pet fish and play music on the radio! There are so many things to do, and it just makes the world feel a lot more lived in!"

CHECK IT OUT!

Scan the code to see **Fraser** in action!

GAME: SURVIVE THE END OF ROBLOX

WHAT IS IT?

"In this game, you're chilling in a beautiful Robloxian city when suddenly disaster strikes, and every bad thing imaginable happens! Buildings collapse, volcanoes erupt, and nukes go off! It's your goal to survive and escape the island!"

BEST BIT!

"My favourite part of the game is the players! A lot of the people who play the game take it very seriously and you can have good fun playing with friends. If – when disaster strikes – one of them gets hit with a boulder, a tear may even fall down your eye! I had a fantastic time playing it and made an awesome friend."

CHECK IT OUT!

Scan the code to see **Fraser** in action!

MAKE A BREAK FOR IT!

YouTube/F2TM

43

ROBLOX VS.

SO RANDOM

No-one wants to get bored playing their fave game, so mixing it up with fresh new modes and fun things to try is key!

ROBLOX
Hundreds of experiences to play through, from obbys to tycoons to battle royales.

FALL GUYS
Brand-new seasons every 2-3 months with new skins, maps and themes.

WINNER: ROBLOX!
As much as we love a fresh Fall Guys update, there are just so many games to choose from that Roblox has to take the W!

AWESOME OBSTACLES

Every epic obstacle course should have a mix of amazing - and challenging - activities that will keep you playing again and again!

ROBLOX
Platform jumps
Fake paths
Lava jumps
Speedruns

FALL GUYS
Hex-A-Gone
Slime Climb
Door Dash
Jump Club

WINNER: FALL GUYS!
Sorry Roblox, as much as we love trying to master 99.999% of your obbies, we know we're going to have so much fun tackling every Fall Guys map – even if we're losing!

FALL GUYS

THE OBBY AWARDS!

LOADSA LOLS

Is there anything greater than a healthy dose of the gaming giggles with your best mates? Nah, we didn't think so either!

ROBLOX

Giant butts, millions of memes, poop parkour... Roblox is home to the silliest of the silly and we love it!

FALL GUYS

From Big Yeetus to funny fails and crazy costumes, Fall Guys is guaranteed to make you laugh out loud!

WINNER: DRAW!

We can't decide! Both games are so hilarious in their own way, it's only fair to call it a tie. Sorry, not sorry!

COOL CUSTOMS

Pick the game that you think has the sickest skins and deserves to take the crown!

WHO'S YOUR WINNER?

ROBLOX   FALL GUYS

BLOXY BINGO

TICK OFF EACH CHALLENGE AS YOU COMPLETE IT!

TOP OF THE BLOX!

- EARNED A BADGE! ☑
- MADE YOUR OWN GAME! ☑
- BEAT YOUR MATES! ☑
- CUSTOMISED YOUR AVATAR! ☑
- DELIVERED A PIZZA! ☑
- FLOWN A HELICOPTER! ☑
- ADOPTED A PET! ☑
- BUILT A HOUSE! ☑
- JUMPED PLAYING PIGGY! ☑
- PLAYED IN AN ELEVATOR! ☑
- COMPLETED AN OBBY! ☑
- STOLEN A CAR! ☑
- BATTLED A MONSTER! ☑
- SPENT AGES PICKING A GAME! ☑
- BUMPED INTO A YOUTUBER! ☑

GET ME OUT OF HERE!

DO

JUMP IN THE CLOSET!

⚠ If you feel a bit scared, look around the room and you're sure to find a closet nearby that you can hide in. But make sure you don't stay too long or you'll get a not-so-friendly visit from the spooky Closet Entity!

TURN AROUND!

⚠ Whenever you're in a dark room and hear a faint voice say "shhh", immediately look in all directions to check for the evil Screech Monster. When you find it, instead of being scared, stare into its eyes and wait for it to get shy and run away!

KEEP YOUR HEAD DOWN!

⚠ When you enter a room and see the iconic glow of the eyes, you should start inspecting your shoes ASAP! Manoeuvre past the creepy fellow and once you're safely out of view, you may raise your head again, knowing that you have successfully made it past that room!

DON'T

STAY BEHIND!

⚠ Playing with friends? Hope you don't need to go to the toilet! If your buddies get 6 rooms ahead of you, then you'll have to encounter the legendary Glitch Entity and he doesn't take too kindly to AFK people!

PANIC!

⚠ Even if things seem super-tough and it looks like there's no way out, there's always something you can do! For example, in the Seek Chase, don't run down a corridor without checking which way the door is – you'll let him catch up easily!

OPEN EVERYTHING!

⚠ If you're fully geared up with flashlights, lockpicks and full health, all you'll be missing out on when searching a drawer is some coins! Opening everything makes the game take ages and you also run the risk of meeting the most dangerous monster of all... TIMOTHY! If you don't listen to this warning, you will greatly regret it!

100 THINGS TO DO IN ROBLOX

100
Take to the skies in Pilot Training Flight Simulator.

99
Get collecting in Pet Simulator X!

98
Give your avatar a cool custom look.

97
Run away from the Piggy!

96
Boss an awesome obby – BACKWARDS!

95
Prepare for a Rob the Bank Obby heist!

94
Build the apartment of your dreams.

93
Race your way through Legends of Speed!

92
Start a private server session with your BFFs!

91
Try Sword Fighters Simulator and boss baddies!

90
Run away from the biggest rat EVER!

89
Sail in a giant rubber duck, SharkBite 2 style!

88
Vroom around the racetrack in Max Speed!

87 Survive Natural Disaster Survival!

86 Avoid the teachers in Escape the School Obby.

85 Steal the cookies without Grumpy Gran catching you!

84 Make a splash and take the W in Big Paintball!

83 Play Elimination Tower and make it all the way.

82 Take to the roads and be a super Taxi Boss!

81 GOOOOOOOAAAAAALLL! Score in Soccer Legends.

CHALLENGE ACCEPTED!

80 Speed Draw your way to arty glory!

79 Brave whatever lies behind the spooky Doors!

78 Brawl it out in Bakugan Battle League.

77 Go bananas and build in Monkey Tycoon!

76 Take on the Easy Obby and jump to victory!

75 Hang out with your mates in Berry Avenue.

74 SHORTEST ANSWER WINS Can you come up with the shortest answer to win?

73

Fend off waves of enemies in All Star Tower Defence!

72

Get 1+ jump power every second!

71

Find your powers in My Hero Mania!

70

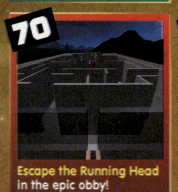

Escape the Running Head in the epic obby!

69

Uncover rare gems in Mining Simulator and find your fortune!

68

Collect and trade legendary pets in Clicker Simulator.

67

Beat bosses and master the Dungeon Quest!

66

Live the high life in Mega Mansion Tycoon!

65

Explore Loooptopia in style!

64

Make every smoothie you can dream of!

63

Become a Zo Samurai and master the art of combat!

62

Uh-oh! Can you escape the flood?

61

Strive to be the best farmer EVER!

60

Show off your top tekkers in TPS: Street Soccer.

BE A BLOX STAR!

59 Rock Color Block and get to the right colour in time!

58 Handle the heat in The Floor is LAVA!

57 Live your best life as a RoCitizen!

56 Head to Roblox Studio and design your own game!

55 Cruise around and earn cash in Car Dealership Tycoon.

54 Share your art with the Spray Paint community!

53 Go to Roblox High School 2 and live it up in Starcadia Bay!

52 Power-up to become a Super Saiyan!

51 Battle spirits and unlock abilities on your Shindo Life adventure!

50 Try out Speed Run Simulator and train for greatness!

49 Get building in Lumber Tycoon 2!

48

Be a hero and build an epic base in **Super Hero Tycoon!**

47

Dress to impress and become **Fashion Famous!**

46

Take on the **MEGA** Challenge!

45

Start a **Driving Empire** and rule the roads!

44

Build, explore and battle bosses, **Grand Piece** style!

43

It's all about **Survival** in this medieval world!

42

Make it out of **Mr Stinky's Detention!**

41

Can you collect fruit and conquer beats in **King Legacy?**

40

Doctor, doctor – cure patients at **Maple Hospital!**

39

Be a real-life hero in **Emergency Hamburg!**

38

Take on the **Boxing League** and battle it out in the ring!

37

Sneak your way to success in **Ninja Legends!**

36

Storm the **Lucky Blocks** Battleground.

35

Cook up delicious meals in **My Restaurant.**

34 Score as many goals as you can in Super Striker League!

33 Either plan or stop a Jailbreak, then fly a helicopter!

32 Join the army to stop the Zombie Uprising!

31 Collect bees to make honey in Bee Swarm Simulator.

30 Check out modes like Skywars and Lucky Blocks in Bedwars!

29 Join Club Roblox, raise pets and play minigames!

28 Play Football Fusion 2 and score a touchdown.

27 Bag an Arsenal of super-cool loot!

26 Own your own dream tropical island!

25 Design a unique Livetopia world!

24 Can you escape the Beast and Flee the Facility?

23 Climb the Epic Minigames leaderboard.

22

Boss Super Golf with a hole-in-one!

21

Explore the wild Mad City Chapter 2!

20

Become a soccer superstar in Touch Football!

19
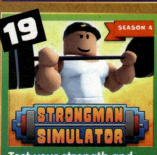
Test your strength and drag items across the line in Strongman Simulator.

18

Build a Boat for Treasure and take to the seas!

17
Face-off in epic Outlaster competitions!

16

Train as a swordsman in Blox Fruits.

15

Can you solve the crimes in Murder Mystery 2?

14
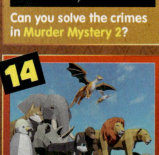
Go wild and discover rare animals in Animal Simulator!

13

Beat the last level of Speed Run 4 as quickly as possible!

12
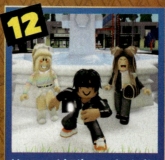
Hang out in the coolest city ever - Brookhaven!

BE A BLOX STAR!

11 Discover everything Greenville has to offer.

10 Go on a rollercoaster ride in Theme Park Tycoon 2.

9 Grow your own dream world in Royale High!

8 Save the world with the Heroes of Robloxia!

7 Chill out in MeepCity and adopt a cute Meep!

6 Enjoy a roleplay adventure in Welcome to Bloxburg!

5 Become a master chef in Restaurant Tycoon 2.

4 Play the most extreme game of Hide and Seek!

3

Explore with mates and create your own awesome world in **Redcliff City**.

2

Adopt, collect and trade the coolest and cutest pets in **Adopt Me!**

SWORDS UP IF YOU'VE DONE ALL 100!

1

Defeat enemies and explore the world of **Swordburst 2!**

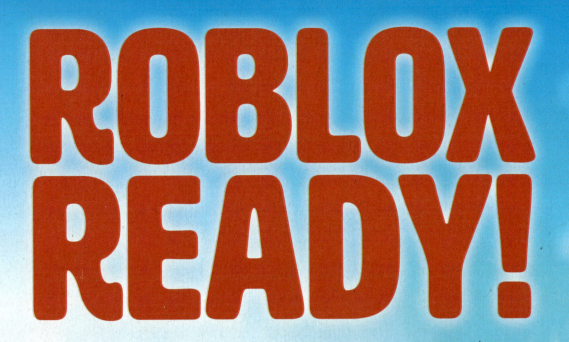

ROBLOX READY!

ROBLOX

THE HOTTEST GAMES RIGHT N[OW]

10

SCUBA DIVING AT QUILL LAKE

■ Explore the mysteries of the ocean and track down curious artifacts in Scuba Diving at Quill Lake. You can explore pirate coves and shark-infested waters, but make sure to avoid toxic waste!

9

ISLANDS

■ Island living isn't all about relaxing! From fighting mobs to building and farming, you'll definitely be kept busy. Packed with resources to collect and items to craft, Minecraft fans will love this!

8

ROYALE HIGH

■ Are you ready for your first day at Royale High? Explore the school, dress up and complete missions to level up. Plus, you can visit different realms, host friends and take part in dance competitions!

4

ADOPT ME!

■ Always wanted a furry (or fanged!) friend, but your parents say no? Roblox is here to help! From dogs to dinosaurs, adopt and take care of your dream pets – or try out adopting a child or being adopted!

3

MEEPCITY

■ Welcome to MeepCity! Here you can hang out and play games, go fishing, create the coolest estates, and even adopt your very own baby Meep. It's all you ever wanted from city-living!

2

WORK AT A PIZZA PLACE

■ Have you not ever dreamt of working at a pizza place? No? Well, maybe you will after playing this insanely fun game! Put your teamwork to the test as you get to grips with everything pizza related!

REPLAY!

W!

7

EPIC MINIGAMES

◻ These minigames really are epic – with over 100 to play, you'll never get bored! Level up every time you win and spend coins on cool effects to make your character awesome!

6

HIDE AND SEEK EXTREME

◻ You can run... and you can hide! If you're 'it' you can use your character's special ability to find the other players. On the flip side, can you find the best places to hide from the seeker and taunt them from afar?

5

SUPER HERO TYCOON

◻ Ever wanted to be Batman or Thor? Play as your favourite superhero and show your might through battle! Build the biggest, coolest base to impress your friends and family!

1
JAILBREAK

◻ The ultimate game of cops and robbers! Will you follow the law and capture some crafty criminals or stage a super heist and make a great escape?

STEALING THE TOP SPOT!

RS

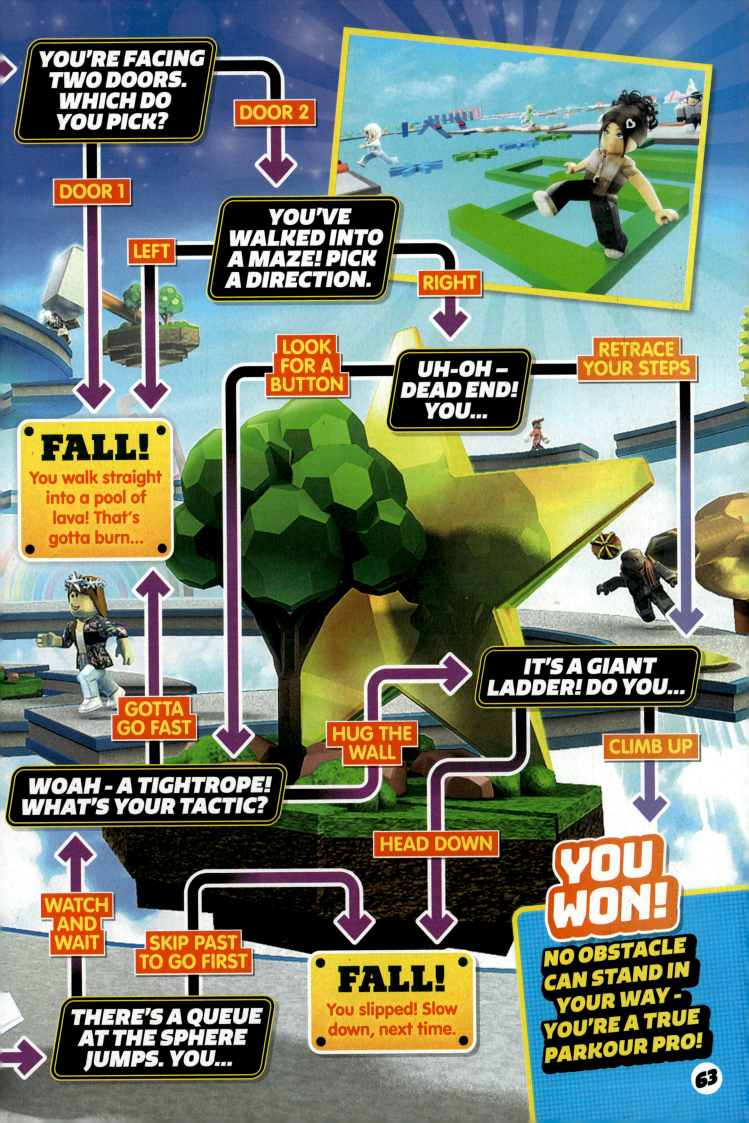

YOU'RE FACING TWO DOORS. WHICH DO YOU PICK?

DOOR 2

DOOR 1

LEFT

YOU'VE WALKED INTO A MAZE! PICK A DIRECTION.

RIGHT

LOOK FOR A BUTTON

UH-OH – DEAD END! YOU...

RETRACE YOUR STEPS

FALL!
You walk straight into a pool of lava! That's gotta burn...

IT'S A GIANT LADDER! DO YOU...

GOTTA GO FAST

HUG THE WALL

CLIMB UP

WOAH - A TIGHTROPE! WHAT'S YOUR TACTIC?

HEAD DOWN

YOU WON!

WATCH AND WAIT

SKIP PAST TO GO FIRST

FALL!
You slipped! Slow down, next time.

NO OBSTACLE CAN STAND IN YOUR WAY - YOU'RE A TRUE PARKOUR PRO!

THERE'S A QUEUE AT THE SPHERE JUMPS. YOU...

63

OBBIES!

OBBIE TYCO

ARE YOU A PARKOUR PRO OR

MEGA FUN OBBY

● With over 2000 different stages to play through, the fun never stops in this obby! How many stages can you beat? You can even check out the sequel, Mega Fun Obby 2, for even more epic levels!

WOAH! NO ONE HAS BAGGED THE STAGE 2730 BADGE YET. CAN YOU?!

ESCAPE THE DENTIST OBBY

● Parkour your way over giant dentures, rivers of toothpaste and more as you make your escape from the evil dentist's office! With obstacles to overcome, puzzles to solve and coins to collect, this obby has a little bit of everything!

FLOOD ESCAPE 2

● Run, jump and dive your way through Flood Escape 2's massive maps! You can play this obby in groups of 12, so it's a great one to get the whole squad involved!

TOP TIP

CHECK OUT FLOOD ESCAPE 2'S TWITTER @ CRAZYBOX_DEV FOR FREE IN-GAME CODES!

IT'S A NICE KNIGHT FOR GAMING!

S VS. ONS!
LLIONAIRE MONEY MAKER?!

TYCOONS!

CLONE TYCOON 2

- It's time to take over the Roblox world! This sci-fi tycoon lets you create an army of clones, kit out a cool base and develop a wicked research lab for all your science experiments!

CAN YOU VISIT THE LAVA PLANET AND FIND ALL THREE KEYS TO UNLOCK THE SUPER-RARE LAVA LAIR BADGE!

THEME PARK TYCOON 2

- Build the theme park of your dreams! As well as loads of awesome rides and roller coasters, there are hundreds of scenery items to pick from to decorate your park exactly how you want.

TOP TIP
DON'T FORGET TO CHECK IN WITH YOUR CUSTOMERS FOR THEIR FEEDBACK!

PIZZA FACTORY TYCOON

- Unleash your inner chef and open your own pizza restaurant! There are loads of crazy toppings to unlock so you can make the coolest pizzas ever!

TOP TIP
UPGRADE YOUR PRODUCTION LINE TO RAKE IN THE DOUGH!

*Figures correct at time of printing.

WHICH TYCOON GAME ARE YOU?

Answer these questions to find out!

CHASE THAT BAG!

YOUR IDEAL DAY OUT WOULD BE...

1 Pizza and pals

2 Hanging out with fam

3 Playing the latest video game

4 SPLAT! Paintball

5 A mega theme park

YOUR FAVOURITE SNACK IS...

1 Pizza

2 Pasta

3 Choccy bars

4 Veggies

5 Candyfloss

OH NO! THERE'S A CAT STUCK IN A TREE! DO YOU...

1 Tempt it down with a snack

2 Leave it – a cat always lands on its feet

3 Ask an adult to help

4 Climb the tree and carry it down

5 Bend the branch so it can climb down

YOUR FAVOURITE COLOUR IS...

1 Red

2 Yellow

3 Blue

4 Green

5 Purple

WORK AT A PIZZA PLACE 4-9

You love food! Particularly pizza, arguably the best snack of all time. Your passion for pizza knows no bounds!

SUPER HERO TYCOON 10-15

You're great at helping others but also kick serious butt too! You're the hero Roblox needs AND deserves!

THEME PARK TYCOON 2 16-20

You're all about the thrills! Through the highs, lows and loop-de-loops, you just want to have tons of fun!

SUPER STRIKER LEAGUE

Super Striker League is an extreme football game that has **Super Smash Bros.** style items which will power-up your player!

Learn when to use which items and it can change the tide of the entire game in an instant! Do really well, and you'll unlock badges and special titles.

CHAMPION!

When you get really confident, you and your friends can take things to Ranked Mode and play against the best of the best!

PLAY NOW!

🟡 The real **Super Striker League** is made exclusively by **Cinder Studio**, so make sure you play that one and avoid any imitators!

BLOX FRUITS

FRUIT MASTER!

THE GAME:
Massive duels... but with edible power-ups!

THE EXTRAS:
▶ Difficult boss fights.
▶ Tricky quests to evolve your skill.
▶ Powerful players for you to fight in the world.

BERRY COOL!

BLOX FRUITS

HOT TIPS:

START SAVING!
This may seem obvious, but don't spend all your money at once! Instead, save up your money to buy much more helpful things, like Fruit!

VISIT THE COUSIN!
On **Jungle Island**, you can find the **Blox Fruits Dealer Cousin**, who'll sell you a random Blox Fruit every two hours. Make sure to check him out, as you could get lucky and get the best fruit in the game for cheaper!

RALLY UP!
Defeating enemies takes lots of time, but if you group them together you can use your abilities to defeat multiple enemies in the time it would take to get rid of one!

RATINGS
Colour in your stats for **Blox Fruits**.

COOLNESS	
SKILL	
FUN	
OVERALL	

WHO WINS? YOU DECIDE!

BEDWARS

BASE BATTLE!

THE GAME:
Survival... but with beds!

BEDTIME!

THE EXTRAS:
- Unique modes such as Skywars.
- Tons of upgrades to give you the upper hand.
- Team modes to play with friends.

BEDWARS

RATINGS
Colour in your stats for **BedWars**.

- COOLNESS
- SKILL
- FUN
- OVERALL

HOT TIPS:

SPEEDRUN!
The start of each round may be the best chance to knock out your enemies as they won't have great gear and may be distracted by getting resources. If you can, rush the enemy ASAP!

SET JOBS AND ROLES!
When playing with friends, try assigning jobs based on what each person is good at. For example, one person can defend the bed while another goes to fight or gather resources.

DOUBLE TROUBLE!
If you want to double the iron and emeralds you earn, wait for a big pile to be on the floor, then stand two blocks away from the generator. Get a friend to collect the loot. Due to a glitch, this'll give you the same amount of loot, too!

MEGA PUZZLES

PUT YOUR PUZZLING SKILLS TO THE TEST!

JAILBREAKERS!
Can you escape Roblox jail?

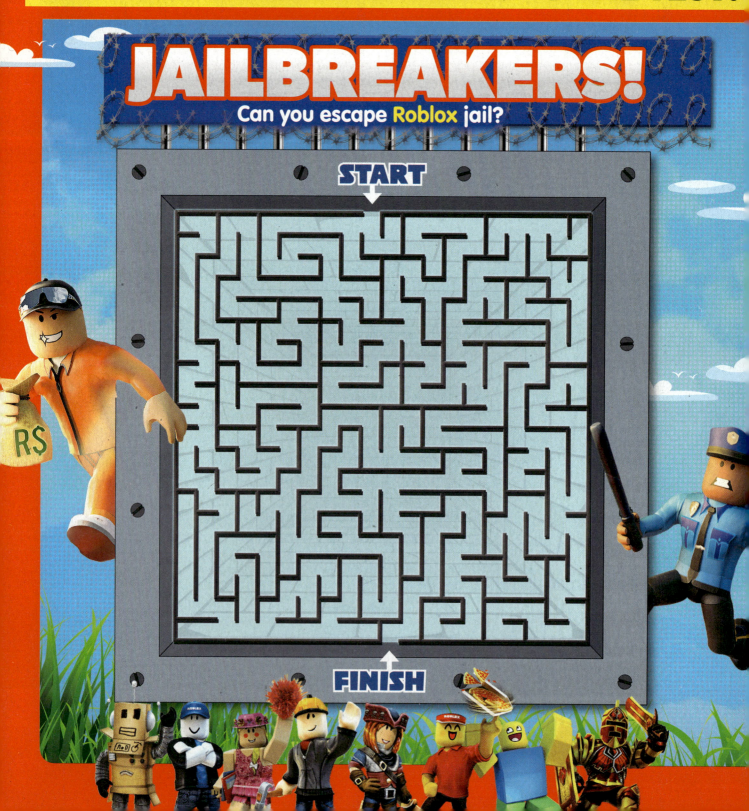

START

FINISH

SPOT THE DIFFERENCE!

Find all five differences between the two pics below!

WORD BLOX!

- GRAVITYCOIL
- HAT
- ROBUX
- OBBY
- GEAR
- AVATAR
- TYCOON
- ROBLOX

```
F L H V H J A V A T A R
G R A V I T Y C O I L D
M T T F R J Q X V Y Y S
B L Y B N W N U U C B F
I U P H J D L B K L S Z
D B T M D H R O B L O X
G I Y S Q E Q R F I I D
B R C Z W K R Y D Q W T
Q R O W B R G E A R J J
L R O Y L G K M R Q H R
Q H N D M P C V Y F E D
T G Q U O B B Y K J J U
```

ODD BLOX OUT!

Which of these is NOT one of the main heroes in Heroes of Robloxia?

- CAPTAIN ROBLOX
- OVERDRIVE
- FAKEBLOX

SPORTS ZONE

BE A SPORTING SUPERSTAR WITH THESE SUPER GAMES!

SUPER GOLF

Take to one of the many cool courses this game has to offer as you work your way up the leaderboards, collecting badges as you go! Will you come out on top with a hole in one or will you bottom out with a bogey?!

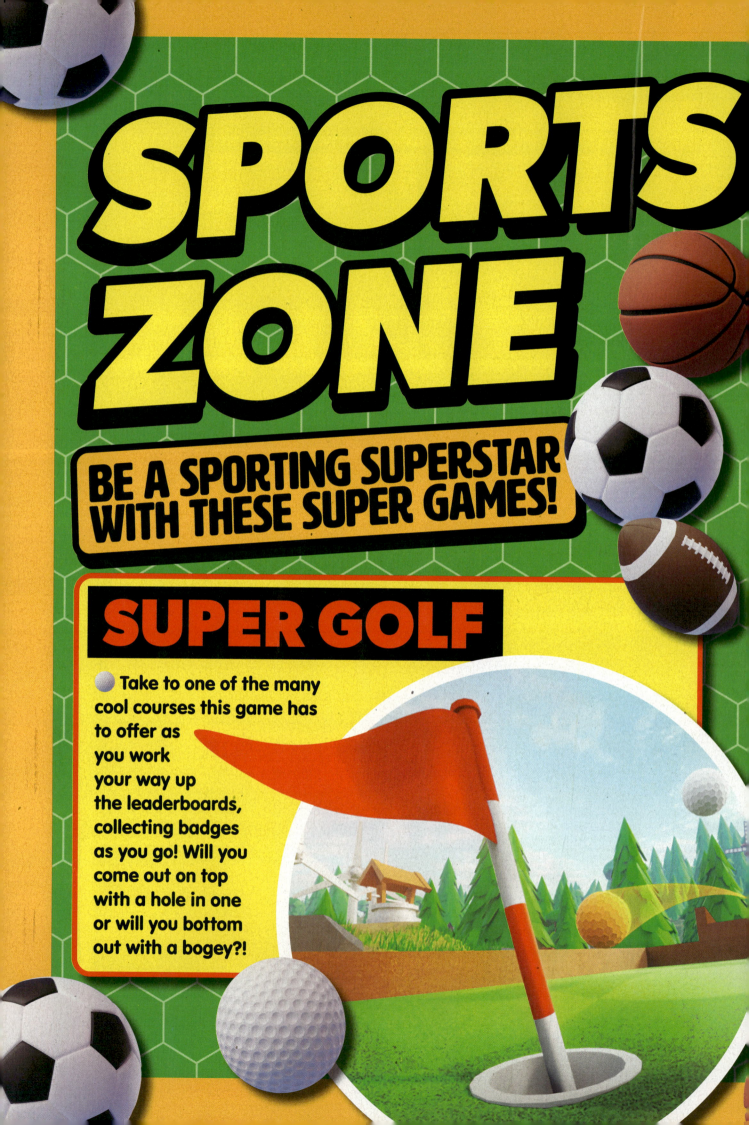

TPS: STREET SOCCER

⚽ Show off your soccer skills in style but watch out – this is no ordinary game of football! With knockouts, power shots and even superpowers, TPS: Street Soccer will put your tekkers to the test like never before.

DUNKING SIMULATOR

🏀 Shoot hoops and slam dunk your way to success on the court! There are loads of awesome jerseys to collect, balls to unlock and even shoes to earn so you can improve your gameplay, range, accuracy and focus in style!

FOOTBALL FUSION 2

🏈 Although some mechanics in this fast-paced football game, like passing, might be tricky to master at first, once you do, you'll be scoring touchdowns and field goals all day long! Plus, there are loads of customisation options, too. TOUCHDOWN!

DODGEBALL

⚪ Duck, dip, dodge and dive to survive in this hard-hitting game! As you battle it out in teams of six vs. six, you'll need to work together, chat to your teammates and come up with solid strategies if you want to snag that W.

SUPER STRIKER LEAGUE

⚽ It's time to take football to the extreme! With epic items to unlock and upgrade, power-ups to master and special abilities to show off, there's never a dull moment in Super Striker League – GOOOAAALLL!

FLEE THE FACILITY!

CAN YOU ESCAPE THIS MAZE?

PIGGY

CAN ANYONE SMELL BACON?

DO

TRICK PIGGY!

⚠️ Many maps provide sneaky escapes to create distance between you and Piggy. Make sure to use these to your advantage when things get tough. On the house map, there's a vent on the top floor that only players can enter, so lure Piggy upstairs and escape through the vent to buy yourself time!

ASSIST ANIMALS!

⚠️ Not all the animals in Piggy are out to get you – some are your friends! For example, on the gallery map, you can give a bone to the dog by the staircase. The dog will return the favour, knocking out Piggy and giving you time to escape!

COMMUNICATE!

⚠️ Capturing all the other players can be difficult when you play as Piggy. However, you have a large array of traps that you can use to slow down, stun or deter players, allowing you to catch up with them. Try to place traps in front of vents or doorways, as players will likely go through those places without looking!

DON'T

STAND STILL !

⚠️ Piggy is always on the hunt – if you're sitting around not paying attention, Piggy will catch up to you and ruin your day! You should always be on the move, looking around for any signs of danger or dead ends.

CHASE IN A STRAIGHT LINE!

⚠️ When you're charging after a player, don't run in a straight line! You and the player run at the same speed, so you'll never catch them. Instead, try cutting them off by going in another direction where you know you'll meet up with them later.

PIGGY'S GONNA GET YOU!

CARRY USED ITEMS!

⚠️ Always swap out your inventory for new and valuable tools and gear to help you solve the puzzles and get away. You don't need used items, so let 'em go and save precious inventory space!

PIGGY

V

PUZZLING PIG!

THE GAME:
Puzzles... but with giant pigs!

THE EXTRAS:

- ▶ An immersive story which will keep you hooked.
- ▶ Loads of unique maps.
- ▶ Challenging game modes keep you on your toes.

YOU'RE BACON ME CRAZY!

HOT TIPS:

BRILL BLUEPRINTS!
You can find blueprints littered throughout different maps – collect them all and you can unlock cool abilities.

VENT AWAY!
In a pickle? Look for a nearby vent and crawl through it to escape the Piggy and buy yourself some extra time!

CUTTING ACROSS!
If you're finding it hard to catch up to players, instead of chasing directly behind them, you could go diagonally to where you think they are going to beat them there!

RATINGS
Colour in your stats for Piggy.

COOLNESS	
SKILL	
FUN	
OVERALL	

WHO WINS? YOU DECIDE!

MURDER MYSTERY 2

MEGA MYSTERY!

THE GAME:
A solvable secret... but with killers!

DID SOMEBODY SAY MURDER?

THE EXTRAS:

▶ Tons of unlockable skins and effects.

▶ Coins scattered throughout the maps.

▶ A **Sheriff** who'll protect you no matter what.

HOT TIPS:

BE THE HERO!
If your **Sheriff** has fallen, have a look to see if you can find their gun on the floor. If you pick it up, you can save the day!

HIDE 'N' SEEK!
Every map has so many hiding spots you can find and chill in to survive the round. Some of them are better hidden than others, so experiment and see what's out there.

THROW THE JAVELIN!
If your victims are really far away, you can throw your knife to hit them. This is especially useful if someone is hiding behind a wall and peeking over to see you!

RATINGS
Colour in your stats for **Murder Mystery 2**.

COOLNESS	
SKILL	
FUN	
OVERALL	

GET CREATIVE!

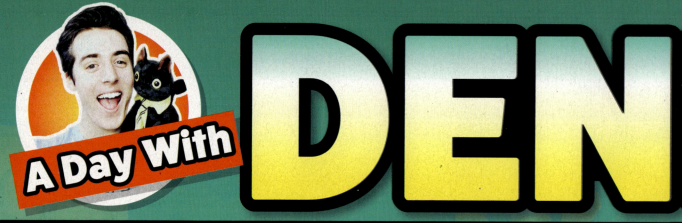

A Day With DENI

We chat Roblox with YouTube superstar, Denis!

Q How did you first discover Roblox?

"When I was younger I would always be browsing the web for fun online minigames. I came across Roblox's Hide & Seek game and I couldn't get enough of it!"

Q Tycoons or Obbies?

"Obbies! Nothing is more exhilarating than speed running through a course and feeling yourself improve every time you practise!"

Q What's the worst Roblox game you've ever played?

"Any Roblox game that tricks you into clicking it! Thankfully, there are a lot less of those now."

I WAS UP GAMING LATE LAST KNIGHT!

S!

★ ★ ★ ★ ★ ★ ★ ★ ★ ★ ★

Q Your biggest YouTube fail?

"One time while playing **Skywars** in **Minecraft**, I dug a hole in a bridge hoping I could trick enemies to fall into it. As I was trying to do this I ended up falling into the hole myself..."

Q Weirdest **Roblox** moment ever?

"Every time you try dancing after applying a baby morph in **Life in Paradise**!"

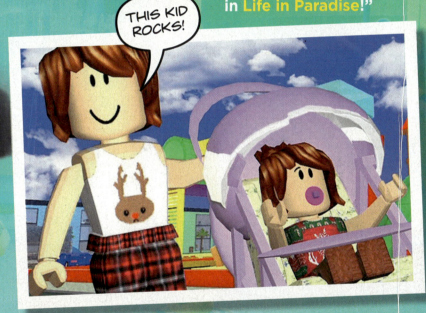

THIS KID ROCKS!

Q Other than **Roblox**, what are your favourite video games?

"I can't get enough of **Rocket League**... it's football, but with cars! What more could you ask for?!"

83

LOOMIAN LEGACY

GOTTA CATCH 'EM ALL!

Catch **Loomians**, train them up, then battle and trade with other players!

Loomian Legacy is a MMORPG (massively multiplayer online role-playing game) experience for monster trainers, with a big world to explore and an adventure to go on!

I'VE LOST MY NOODLE!

If you're really good at raising monsters, you should take on the Battle Theatre challenge. Will you collect all the medals?

PLAY NOW!

🔸 Watch out for imposters! **Loomian Legacy** is by **Llama Train Studio**, so that's the version to look for!

85

110% GAMING

GET YOUR FIRST 3 ISSUES FOR £7!*

SAVE ON SHOP PRICE!

WHY SIGN UP?

★ Get all the latest gaming news first!

★ Every issue delivered straight to your door before it hits the shops!

★ Amazing free gifts in every issue!

ASK AN ADULT TO

SUBSCRIBE HERE!

WHAT TO DO...

ONLINE
Ask an adult to help. Visit our website at 110gaming.com and choose 'payment option'.

OR

BY PHONE
Ask an adult to help. Call free on 0800 318846 (Mon-Fri 8am-6pm).

QUOTE 110RB

*Direct Debit offer for new customers only. £7 for the first three months, then £15 every three months. 110% Gaming is a monthly title publishing 12 issues per year. Prices shown are based on UK delivery and are correct at the time of going to print. Offers are subject to change.

WELCOME TO BLOXBURG

COOL CITY!

THE GAME:
Life... but you can build your own house!

Welcome to **Bloxburg**

HOME, SWEET HOME!

THE EXTRAS:

▶ Tons of customisable decorations.

▶ Hard-working jobs to earn all the cash.

▶ Pesky bills that you keep forgetting to pay.

HOT TIPS:

BULLDOZE!
If you aren't happy with the look of your house and want to restart, make sure to use the bulldoze tool as it'll save way more time clearing your plot than selling everything individually.

DRESS HOW YOU WANT!
If you want to change the clothes your character wears without spending Robux, then you can use the dressers or wardrobes in the game but remember, you don't get to keep them!

PRECISION IS KEY!
Struggling to place things where you want them? By using the grid tool, you can make your decorations more precise so they go exactly where you want them to!

RATINGS Colour in your stats for **Welcome To Bloxburg**.

COOLNESS
SKILL
FUN
OVERALL

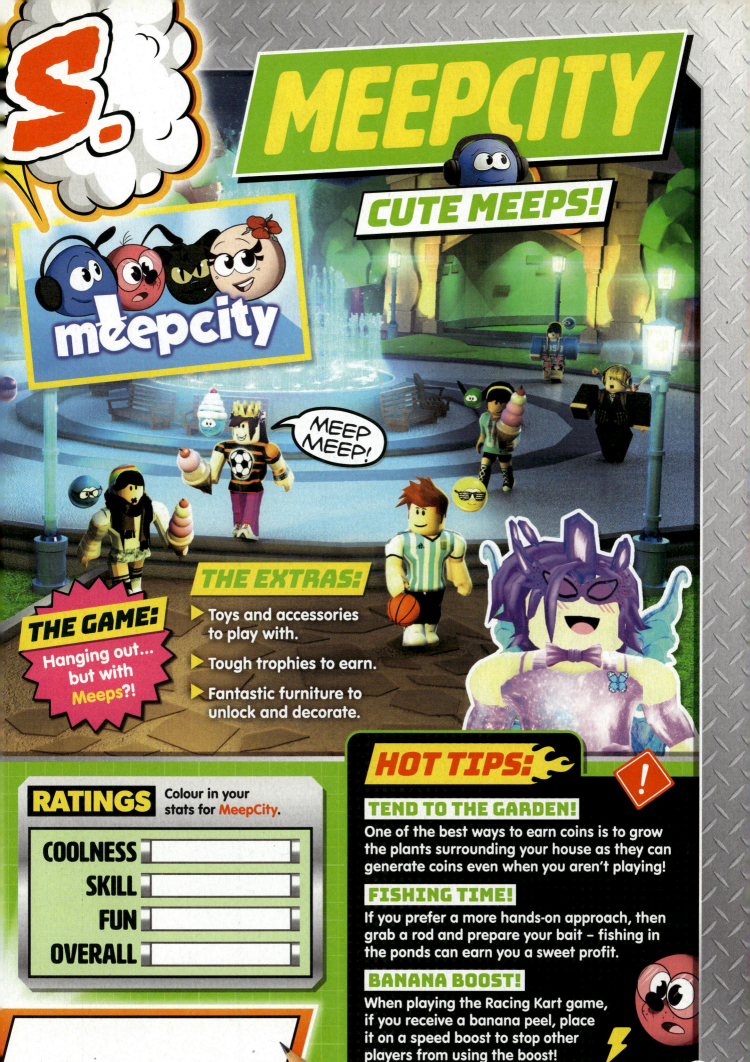

MEEPCITY

CUTE MEEPS!

meepcity

MEEP MEEP!

THE EXTRAS:

- Toys and accessories to play with.
- Tough trophies to earn.
- Fantastic furniture to unlock and decorate.

THE GAME:

Hanging out... but with Meeps?!

RATINGS

Colour in your stats for MeepCity.

COOLNESS	
SKILL	
FUN	
OVERALL	

HOT TIPS:

TEND TO THE GARDEN!

One of the best ways to earn coins is to grow the plants surrounding your house as they can generate coins even when you aren't playing!

FISHING TIME!

If you prefer a more hands-on approach, then grab a rod and prepare your bait – fishing in the ponds can earn you a sweet profit.

BANANA BOOST!

When playing the Racing Kart game, if you receive a banana peel, place it on a speed boost to stop other players from using the boost!

IT'S A JAILBREAK!

CAN YOU FIGHT YOUR WAY TO FREEDOM?

START

WHAT'S YOUR GETAWAY RIDE? —— **SUPERCAR**

THE ALARM GOES AND YOUR CELL OPENS! YOU HEAD FOR...

A SECRET TUNNEL

TIME FOR A SNEAKY DISGUISE. WHAT DO YOU PICK?

MOTORBIKE

PIZZA DELIVERY GUY

FIND A NEW RIDE

THE DOOR

YOU ZIP PAST A POLICE CAR, BUT IT SEES YOU! YOU...

CAUGHT!
The door is surrounded by guards, silly!

SPEED UP

CAUGHT!
The police radio shared your description, and the next cops recognised you!

CAUGHT!
The pizza smelled so yummy you stopped for a quick bite – mistake!

YOU'RE NICKED!

GIMME A PIZZA THAT!

MAKE A U-TURN

CAUGHT!
You come face-to-face with a wall of cop cars – there's no escape!

UH-OH – ROADBLOCKS AHEAD! YOU...

SMASH THROUGH

DITCH IT

NOW YOU'RE ON FOOT! YOU...

YOU MADE IT! BUT THE CAR'S PRETTY BANGED UP...

KEEP GOING

STICK TO THE STREETS

HIT THE ROOFTOPS

LEFT

WILD WEST COWBOY

THE ALLEY SPLITS IN TWO! WHICH WAY?

I'M BLOCK-BUSTING OUTTA HERE!

RIGHT

R$

YOU ESCAPED!

A GETAWAY PLANE WAS WAITING ON THE ROOF. TIME TO FLY TO FREEDOM!

YOU FOUND THE PIZZA PLACE'S FIRE ESCAPE! YOU...

GO INSIDE

CLIMB UP

READY TO RACE!

VROOM! THESE ROBLOX RACERS ROCK!

VEHICLE LEGENDS

With cars, motorbikes, boats, planes and even helicopters, there are loads of ways to race around in style! Plus, the more you race, the more money you earn so you can buy even more epic vehicles to add to your collection.

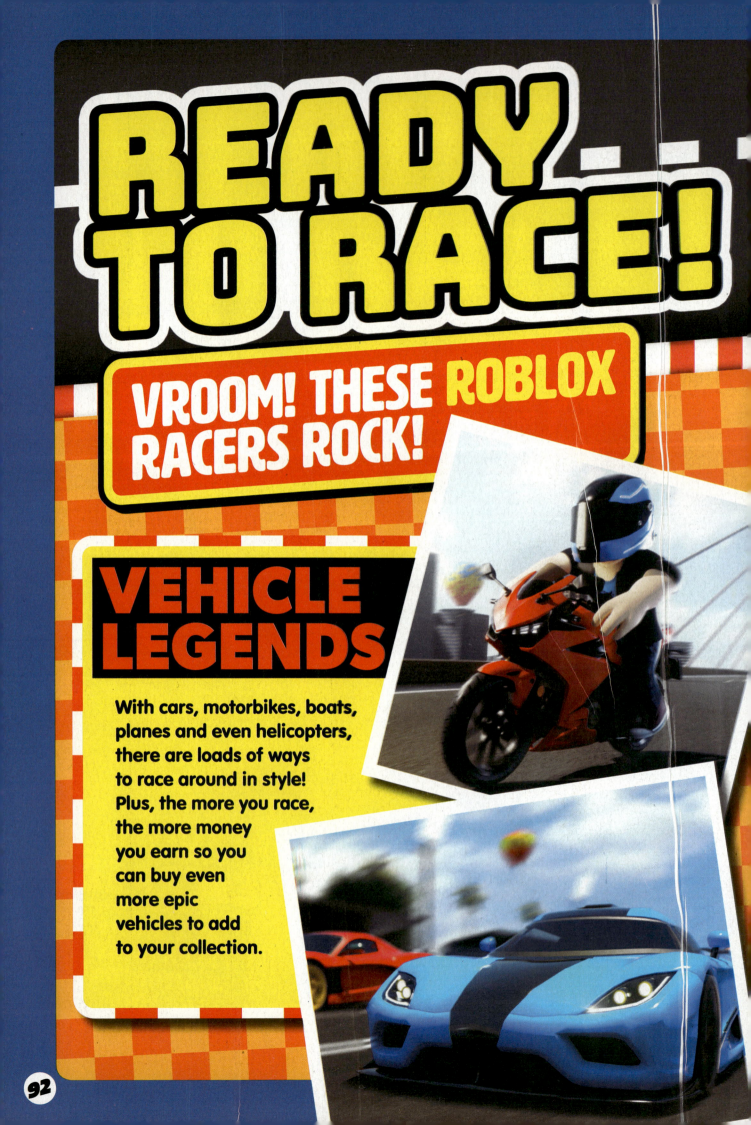

DRIVING EMPIRE

Hit the road in this epic simulator for a driving experience that feels just like the real thing! With over 250 super-sick rides to choose from, as well as the ability to customise each car, you can really make this racer your own.

HOT WHEELS OPEN WORLD

Get the official **Hot Wheels** experience as you race around one of the biggest ever maps on **Roblox**! There are so many epic vehicles to check out, as well as loads of awesome quests to go on and epic stunts to perform!

MIDNIGHT RACING: TOKYO

Explore this epic recreation of Tokyo as you race through streets, motorways and mountains! There are over 130 different cars for you to collect and you can even tune each one to your own driving style, so you're sure to have the edge in any race.

ION FORMULA RACING

If you love Formula 1, this game is for you! Join one of 20 different teams to build and develop your own race car, competing and racing all over the world. With different weather conditions, car damage, slipstreams and more, this is one of the most realistic Roblox racers around!

DRIFT PARADISE

This arcade-style racer might be tricky to master at first, but when you do, it's so rewarding! Once you've got the hang of drifting and gliding through corners, you'll be able to take on any track with confidence, racing your way to victory!

SPOT THE DIFFERENCE!

■ THERE ARE FIVE SNEAKY DIFFERENCES BETWEEN THESE TWO PICS. CAN YOU FIND THEM ALL?

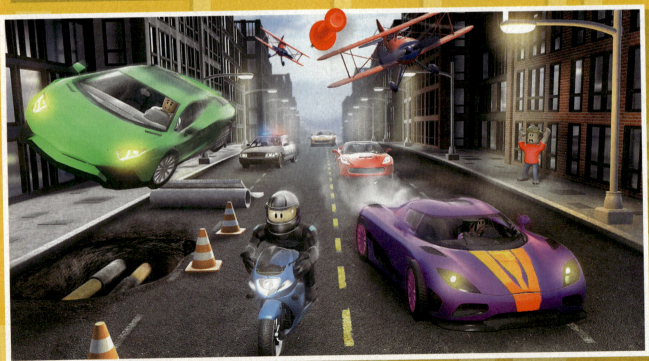

ANSWER

96

PICK ME, PICK ME!

ADOPT ME!

DO ⚠

THE TRADING QUIZ!

⚠ Securing your collection's safety is vital so head over to the Safety Hub and take the quiz to make sure you're aware of all the sneaky tricks scammers will try! As a reward, you can unlock a trade license, letting you swap with others and view your trading history.

STAY IN THE GAME! ⚠

⚠ Earning cash in Adopt Me! can be a slow and challenging task but you can sometimes earn 20 Bucks just for playing! You don't even have to be active to earn it – as long as you check in every 20 minutes to avoid being kicked out. You could watch a movie or go for a short walk and still earn AMC!

KNOW YOUR WORTH!

⚠ Some pets aren't available for very long, making them rarer and harder to get. These are usually worth more so avoid trading them for something less valuable. A quick way to check an item's value is by looking at its rarity in your inventory. If your pet can fly, be ridden, is an adult or a neon, that can also add to its value! ⚠

DON'T

TRUST TRADE! ⚠

⚠ 'Trust trades' are when you trade your item for something worth a lot less with the promise that they'll give you something worth a lot more after. This is often a scam so if someone asks to do one, ignore them and walk away!

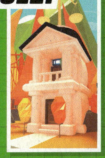

RUSH PEOPLE!

⚠ If you're in a trade and the other person is taking a lot of time to decide whether to accept, don't tell them to hurry up. Sometimes people need to think, especially if it's a high-value trade. The best thing to do is wait; maybe you'll end up with a better deal than before! ⚠

BUY FOOD!

⚠ Your pets need to eat which can cost a lot of money. However, instead of buying an expensive pizza, you could head to the school and stock up on free apples! It's healthier and helps you save up for a cool vehicle, a new pet or a fancy house!

DID YOU KNOW?

COLOSSAL COLLECTION!

In **Adopt Me!**, there are over 300 different pets and eggs to collect! How many do you have?

GAMES GALORE!

Thanks to **Roblox Studio**, anyone can make their own game. In fact, there are over 40 MILLION playable experiences on **Roblox**!

HOT HAT!

Although there are hundreds of hat options for your avatar, the rarest of them all is the **Kleus Aphthiton** – only four players have a real one!

NEW NAME!

Roblox wasn't always called **Roblox**! In its early days, it was actually called **DynaBlocks**!

MONEY MAKER!

If your creations are successful, you can earn money making **Roblox** games! The **Roblox Corp** paid out over £400,000,000 to creators in a single year.